G000155007

The Internet for Managers

RRC Penfold

NET-WORKS

**PO BOX 200
Harrogate
HG1 2YR
England**

**www.net-works.co.uk
Email: sales@ net-works.co.uk
Fax: +44 (0) 1423 526035**

Net.Works is an imprint of Take That Ltd

ISBN: 1-873668-88-0

10 9 8 7 6 5 4 3 2 1

Contents

Introduction

With the possible exception of the first Moon landing, no technology has excited so much public interest and media coverage as the Internet. Everyone is using it, talking about it or signing up for it - apparently. The only problem is, despite massive improvements, the Internet is still a strange place full of previously unheard jargon, acronyms and initials. All of which is more than a little unfortunate for the hard-pressed manager who, somehow, has to make sense of it all.

In point of fact there is nothing strange or mysterious about the Internet (although that can describe some of the people who use it). Just look on it as a, relatively, new medium of communication and all the rest falls into place. In other words ignore the hype and forget all talk about such things as cyberspace if only because hype only rarely has any basis in reality and cyberspace owes everything to a work of fiction.

The term was first used by William Gibson in his novel 'Neuromancer' to describe a place where people met each other electronically after physically plugging themselves into a computer terminal. There were no Personal Computers in the novel, or any other of the paraphernalia of modern Information Technology. It just happened, although, strangely, in Gibson's dismal version of the future the only reason why people ventured into cyberspace was to steal data from other computers. (Perhaps the story was prophetic after all.)

Back in real life the Internet is just a gigantic collection of computers all joined together. Some companies can find a use for it while for others it will be a complete waste of time; the trick is to know which is which. For that reason alone there can only be one sensible course of action: ignore the evangelists, ignore the doomsayers; find out what it all means, how it works and why. Then come to a rational decision based on cold, hard, logic. The people who throw around words like cyberspace or cyber culture the way their parents once used words like psychedelic might not be too pleased, but, unless they are paying the bills, who cares. Where company money is concerned better to be a slow developer than a fashion victim.

To put that another way. Companies may claim to be thinking about using the Internet and yet no company thinks about launching a new product or investing in new equipment. If a solid business case can be made they go ahead and do it. If not, not. So with the Internet which should be treated no differently. Either its use can be supported with financial arguments or else it becomes an expensive luxury in which case the decision is already taken. Like the new product or the new equipment its use has to be justified, which can only be done when, all the facts are known. Therefore, learn the facts, check the costs, understand the pitfalls and consider the implications.

In other words, read this book.

For those hard pressed for time, or without the patience to wade through too much theory, the practical aspects are dealt with first. In this way everything from establishing the business objectives of a website, to the technical issues involved or the marketing of that website are covered immediately. After that, for those who want to know more, such things as the history of the Internet or the way governments are reacting to an increasingly online world are covered in a series of appendices.

To some these appendices may not be as important as the process of establishing a web commerce venture, but they should still be read. In a world where information is increasingly being seen as a tangible asset, information about the Internet might just be the most important asset of all.

Chapter One

Why Go Online?

Establish your business objectives in going online. According to some reports the entire world will soon be online. There are even those who insist no company will be able to survive without its own website and still more are predicting the end of the traditional, bricks and mortar, organisation. Add to that statements about how the Internet is the biggest revolution in mass communication since the invention of the printing press and it soon becomes obvious something special has happened.

So what is the Internet all about and why are so many claims being made for it?

To answer that the best thing to do would be to inject a note of reality into the proceedings. Firstly bear in mind that most of these comments stem from people who have a vested interest in the subject. Be they software manu-facturers, hardware manufacturers, web design agencies or Internet Service Providers they all intend to make money out of everyone else trying to make money by going on-line. Whether anybody else will make money is a different matter altogether, but these people will - and already do.

Next comes the question of how anyone can claim the entire world will one day be wired up which is very easily answered. It comes from a faulty reading of the statistics. True the growth of the Internet has been explosive to say the least, but all that happened in the past. Any claim that the future will be a simple straight-line extension of what has already happened should be viewed cautiously in the extreme.

As proof try applying that same logic to a few historical events.

◆   In the 1890's it would have proved that today Britain would rule the world. (Look at the growth of the British Empire.)

- In the 1940's it would have proved that today everyone would be living in the greater German Reich ruled over by the Nazis. (Look how fast they dominated Europe.)

- In the 1960's it would have proved that today America would dominate the world. (Look at the strength of its economy.)

- In the 1980's it would have proved that by today Japan would have bought the world. (Look at the strength of its economy.)

Add to that other comments made about the Asian tiger economies on the Pacific Rim (until they had to be bailed out by the IMF) and it soon becomes obvious that the past is a very poor indicator of the future. History is always being changed by circumstances, which no one saw at the time, but which are clearly visible when looked at with hindsight. That being the case the best idea of all would be to try and spot these circumstances before the event instead of waiting for hindsight to set in. Then sensible decisions can be taken. Even so, as changing circumstances are notoriously difficult to detect, that still leaves a problem, which can perhaps best be solved by looking at some of the myths surrounding the Internet.

In no particular order these are:

No Company Will Be Able to Survive Without a Website

Anyone who claims this should be asked if they buy their morning newspaper or petrol for their car at the newsagent or filling station most convenient or the one with the best website. Should that be too trivial ask if anyone has ever refused to watch the latest Hollywood movie simply because it had no associated website. Alternatively, who has ever refused to eat at a particular restaurant or drink in a particular pub for no better reason than because there was no trace of it on the Internet.

There are any number of businesses continuing to trade successfully without any thought of the Internet and this will be true no matter how wired up the rest of the world becomes. Admittedly some of these are part of larger organisations who in all probability will have a website, but only as a small part of their overall business strategy not as a means of survival. The idea that a major oil company or brewery would collapse for lack of a website is laughable.

On the plus side, of course, there are companies which thrive on the Internet. To be more accurate they thrive because of the Internet. These are the small companies who, for the first time ever, are able to compete on level terms with their much bigger rivals. No longer does the business go to the company with the biggest marketing budget. Now the possession of a website means any company has a global presence.

In fact it is this that makes some people claim a website is necessary for survival. If small companies can take business away from big companies, which they can, then it follows that big companies must also have a website or else forever lose business. In other words everybody needs a website.

It has to be said there is some truth to this. Small companies can take business away from big companies thanks entirely to the Internet. The trick is in knowing where this applies. As already mentioned some companies will never need a website, others will. Once that is accepted decisions can be made.

Soon All Business Will be Done On-Line

If so it has yet to be proved. A case in point is the Argos shopping chain which set up business on the Internet in 1995; nine months later it had sold just twenty-two items. Not that this should be seen as a surprise, according to a report by the major consultancy firm GarnerGroup (released in November 1999) 75% of all on-line ventures fail. However the report did go on to state 'The companies which succeed, from both the traditional and start-up background, will have worked out what is reality and what is hype.' An opinion which could almost be described as the theme of this book.

Obviously there are some businesses which can thrive in the on-line environment. One such is Comic Shack which was facing bankruptcy when it traded from a single shop, but which has since gone from strength to strength when it started selling its comics over the Internet. Interestingly the owner, David Shack, was in his sixties when he started his e-commerce venture. There is no ageism on the Internet.

A further example of this is the holiday industry where an increasing number of people are booking their holidays over the Internet instead of through a travel agent. Presumably they think that as the travel agent in effect books their package holiday using a computer link they might as well do it for themselves and cut out the middle man. (A process referred to by Internet analysts as disintermediation.)

As for other companies; at a time when TV shopping channels have been available for years and catalogue shopping has been around for decades the sheer number and variety of retail outlets must say something about the way people prefer to spend their money. The Internet is unlikely to change that no matter how popular it gets. A fact which also holds true for companies not in the retail trade. There the standard methods of doing business will still be as valid.

Here it is worth mentioning a comment occasionally made by some companies to the effect that in future they will only be doing business over the Internet. With the exception of companies which are totally Internet creations, like on-line banks for example, all companies must still be able to cater for those customers who have no Internet connection. This must be obvious. Are they really suggesting they would turn down an order simply because the buyer had no Internet account? Would they really buy from a supplier who had a website in preference to one who offered better price, delivery and quality, but had no presence on the World Wide Web?

If the answer to these questions is yes perhaps the best advice is to insist on cash only transactions when dealing with them. Why risk becoming an unsecured creditor when they inevitably go bankrupt.

Back in the real world comments like that tend to be made by companies with a major financial stake in persuading other people to go on-line. It is not a mission statement nor is it a statement of intent. It is just a company with a major presence trying to use, or abuse, their position in the market for further gain and it should be treat as such.

Better yet, the next time someone makes a statement like that ask them about their plans to lay off their entire sales force. The answer should be more instructive than anything else they have to say.

The Customer Base Will Be Expanded

What this means is that by having a website where orders can be placed new business can be picked up fairly painlessly. While this is true there is an old accountant's saying that should be remembered: 'Turnover equals vanity; Profits equals sanity'. If the cost of doing business over the Internet is more than the profit it generates then what is the real value of that business?

This is the aspect of Internet life most quoted by those people trying to sell their particular (web related) service. Usually the example given is of a speciality baker or butcher (for reasons unexplained butchers seem to be favourite) except when the example is looked at in any detail the amount of business generated by the Internet is a tiny fraction of the overall turnover. Also remember that these companies deal directly with the public who buy in small amounts and pay by credit card secure in the knowledge that, should there be a problem, the credit card company will refund them. Away from that line of work businesses who went on-line hoping for bigger orders from other companies have a very different story to tell.

Here the success story usually quoted is Dell Computers who set up their own website - and in less than thirty-six months sales from that site amounted to over $1 billion. However, the other computer manufacturers fared differently because, while they too wanted to sell over the Internet, they also had their established retailers and dealers to consider. (Being a mail order company Dell had no such worries.)

This highlights a problem any company could have because those retailers and dealers were still needed even after the Internet business was established and yet no dealer would be prepared to accept the loss of business that would inevitably follow if the website could offer a better deal than them.

In practice this meant that the website had to offer no special incentive to prospective customers just to protect the more standard retail outlets. This was obviously important and should serve as a warning to any other companies. Even in the case of Dell the Internet trade accounted for just 15% of its turnover with the other manufacturers recording even less, making those dealers that much more important.

Support Costs Will Be Reduced

The argument here is that instead of having to pay for promotional literature or catalogues and then pay even more to maintain telephone support lines all the information can be published on the World Wide Web. That way anyone who needs a new catalogue, for example, could download the latest, constantly updated, version of it.

Similarly if they need help the answers to the most common problems could be stored on a web page to be viewed at their leisure. (In the language of the Internet they would be called FAQ's or Frequently Asked Questions.)

While all of this is true the chance of anyone being able to reduce their support costs is practically zero. Customers will still want sales brochures and no one can rely on them having an Internet account so they will still have to be printed - and paid for. In much the same way anyone with a problem not covered by the web page, or, again, without an Internet account will still need telephone support.

From this it follows that, rather than fall, service costs will actually rise by the price of keeping that web page. Against this, of course, is the fact that the number of support calls might decrease (and the operative word is might) which means less people would be needed to handle them. That would, naturally, reduce support costs, but as no one could predict or calculate these savings it would be better not to expect them.

Even so, while a website might not reduce the cost of service it would undoubtedly increase the level of that service. By being available on what is usually referred to as a 24x7 basis (twenty-four hours a day, seven days a week) a website with its most common questions and answers, FAQ's, would be available to any customer well outside normal office hours.

New Suppliers Will Be Found

A simple search through the Internet might find alternative suppliers capable of providing a better degree of service than those currently being used. This is true, but those same suppliers should also be in everything from trade directories to the yellow pages which makes the value of searching the Internet entirely debatable.

New Ways of Working Will Be Found

This is also true to a certain extent. Some companies already have data processing centres in the third world who then transmit the processed information over phone lines to the European or American head office. This obviously gives any company doing it the advantage of lower labour costs, but as it is usually done over dedicated phone lines no one can really claim that the Internet is involved.

To be more accurate they should claim it an as example of electronic communication (which is totally separate from the Internet) although few people are prepared to make that distinction.

Away from such heady heights it is true to say that the easy access to information which a company website provides, plus the communication facilities suddenly available through email can make small satellite offices a much more viable proposition. Because of this a new office could be set up in any part of the world, no matter how remote, and yet still be fully integrated into the corporate structure.

Alternatively one large office responsible for company activities over a wide geographical area could be split into much smaller branch offices covering less ground, but being equally a part of the corporate mainstream.

The Corporation Will Cease to Exist

This is one of those apocalyptic visions so beloved by the media. The idea is that soon everybody will work from home and communicate entirely by email so there will be no need for company offices, or even physical contact. Very often this is given a political spin by the commentators concerned who are more anxious to discuss the disintegration of society than the practicalities of the situation.

To them the only aspects worth considering are how people will be deprived of human contact, and therefore unable to form any kind of society, or the division of the world into the disenfranchised poor who have no access to the technology or the so-called information rich, invariably described as the Alphas. (Another term which owes everything to a work of fiction. In this case Aldous Huxley's 'Brave New World' although the people who use such terms would be well advised to read the book, if only to see what Huxley was writing about.)

Needless to say any such posturing should be regarded as the politics it undoubtedly is and ignored by anyone intent on living in the real world. In practical terms it will never happen; all companies rely on ad hoc meetings or the fact that people will be immediately available to answer a question or help solve a problem. Take that away and the only way the corporation would cease to exist would be caused by bankruptcy not technology.

For anyone still not convinced the remedy is simple. Next time some newspaper or magazine publishes an article along these lines write to the editor asking how far advanced their plans are for dismantling the company. Given that media organisations, and those in the print industry particularly, should be prime candidates for this treatment as articles and editorials can be sent in electronically the answer should be illuminating.

By now anyone reading this could be thinking that it is fanatically opposed to the Internet when nothing could be further from the truth. The Internet can be a fascinating place in its own right and a business opportunity so full of potential that everyone has to take it seriously. Having studied it they might decide it is unsuitable for their company or ways of working, but they still must seriously consider it.

In fact the entire point of this book is exactly that: the serious study of the Internet and its application as a business tool.

For that reason the myths had to be destroyed, or at least put into a proper perspective, so that any decisions taken could have a rational basis and no-one would be taken in by what is to a certain extent misinformation and industry hype.

In fact there are many reasons why a company might want to join what is usually described as the Internet community. Any one of them alone could totally justify the expenditure involved although as the various levels of service available each call for a different level of expense it might be a good idea to know just what these options are. Then sensible decisions can be taken.

email

Although basically a method of passing messages from one computer to another email is becoming increasingly popular, in part because those computers sending messages to each other could be in adjacent offices or on opposite sides of the world. In fact the ability to send a letter or memo halfway across the world at the speed of electricity instead of the more traditional postal services is one of the strengths of the Internet. Because of email even the remotest office can maintain practically instant communication with headquarters, or even another remote office.

It is even possible for individuals, or individual departments, within a company to have their own email addresses, something like sales@ companyname.co.uk or jsmith@companyname.com. Fairly obviously any message sent to such an address would go directly to the department or individual concerned which can do wonders for corporate efficiency. If database or spreadsheet reports are currently printed out by one office, posted and then have to be manually re-entered by whatever office receives them then the time taken to re-enter that data is the only true cost saving for email. There the database or spreadsheet file could be sent electronically and so be ready for use immediately without the need to re-enter that data. A saving obviously, but not enough to justify Internet access by itself.

Perhaps the problem with email is that, while it increases efficiency, its benefits are very often hard to quantify. As such it should be seen as an additional advantage to be considered alongside other reasons for going on-line. (email is discussed in more detail in Appendix D)

Internet Searches

In terms of complexity this is the next step up from email. There is no website to think about, or pay for, the costs are obvious and strictly controllable and the ISP will provide an email address to each of its subscribers. It might be treating the so-called information superhighway more like a one-way street, but if the company needs, or can afford, no more then why argue.

There is a massive amount of information to be found on the Internet, a signif-icant percentage of which is valid for the business user. The Sales department could use it to track down potential new customers, always assuming these new customers have their own websites. For example a company making components for, say, diesel engines could use the Internet to trace every diesel engine manufacturer in the world (or on the Internet at least).

After that they could be contacted either by email or by more conventional means and business might be done. In much the same way the Purchasing Department could find new suppliers although this is probably only useful if rare or specialist material is needed. With the number of local, national and international trade directories currently available any suppliers of standard components are unlikely to need the Internet before they can be contacted. (Even so, if a case can be made for Internet access then cancelling the subscription payments to a few trade directories and switching to on-line searches could be a valid cost saving.) It should also be said that this makes the case for any supplier of specialist goods or services to have their own website.

Away from such obvious examples there is also information for the business traveller, information regarding the viability and credit rating of new cust-omers and suppliers can be found as can any amount of specialist information which the technical departments might need - all of it instantly available at the press of a button. In fact probably every department could find a reason to use the Internet so the only real question is, could the cost be justified?

As in any other new project that will always be the stumbling block although as Internet access at this level is extremely cheap it should be seriously considered. (Searching the Internet is discussed in more detail in Appendix D)

Company Websites

This is where a company acquires a presence on the Internet as opposed to being merely a visitor. With its own website even the smallest company can be the equal of a giant multi-national, on the Internet at least. In a world where physical size is impossible to judge, and anyway irrelevant, all companies are equal. Better yet the opportunities for business on the Internet are just as equally dispersed so there could be rich pickings for everyone - all they have to do is own a website.

Unfortunately in the real world nothing is ever that simple. To begin with questions have to be asked about what type of website the company will own; closely followed by who will pay for it. Then other, related, questions can be considered such as who will do it, what will they do and how much can they spend on doing it. All of which have to be answered as the cost of a company website can vary enormously depending entirely on what the website will be used for. It therefore makes sense to first of all consider the differences between the various types of websites and from there decide who will pay for it and how much should be allocated to the project.

Advertising

This is a website at its simplest. Here a company does nothing more than show its name, address, perhaps its logo and a description of what it does. It could best be described as the reverse of an Internet search; creating a website for others to find. Most Internet Service Providers offer a certain amount of free space on their computers where web pages can be stored as part of the basic package they offer to new subscribers so the only cost involved, other than the monthly subscription, is the cost of creating the web page in the first place. Exactly how much that is likely to be obviously depends on whether it is done in-house or through a web design agency and how elaborate those web pages will be, but it should not cost too much. The website is just not complex enough for it to be expensive.

Of course the amount of new business it generates is entirely problematical. Like all advertising its effectiveness can sometimes be difficult to judge, but at least the cost of it is easy to allocate; by definition it should come out of the advertising budget.

Information

This is much more complex, both to create and describe. In part this is because the term 'information' can have such a wide range of meanings that one single explanation is practically impossible. It could even be argued that an advertising website is information as it informs the Internet world about the existence of the company who owns it and, just to make matters even more confusing, if an information website carries the company name and logo - which it very likely will - then that could be counted as advertising.

Because of this the best way of dealing with the subject is to break it down into various categories, each one to be discussed separately.

Customer Care

Some companies offer telephone support lines where customers experiencing problems with whatever product the company is selling can call for help and advice. The Internet equivalent of this is a customer care website. By creating a website where all the most common problems are listed together with their causes and solutions a company can offer a much improved service to their customers as this website, in fact any website, would be open twenty-four hours a day, making the information available outside of normal office hours. Better than that anyone using the website would have no worries about being stuck in a seemingly endless queue waiting for their call to be answered by a human operator.

There are those who claim this will also reduce costs in that the more people use the Internet so the less they will call the customer help lines leading to fewer operators being needed and fewer telephone lines although, if true, this has yet to be proved. In the short term at least no savings will be made, nor should any be expected. Initially it is highly unlikely there will be any reduction in the volume of calls to the help line and it is far from guaranteed even in the medium term. Perhaps in the long term a customer care website will have a noticeable effect on the help line, but it would be unwise to plan for it.

The good news is that such a website could be constructed relatively easily. Any company needing to operate help lines is already likely to have a list of the most common questions set up in some form of computerised database (and if not one could be created without too much effort). This could obviously be used to form the basis of the website, in some cases with practically no modification.

Even if the computerised database still needs more work before it can be converted into a website at the very least just by owning it the company will know how big it is and, therefore, how much space needs to be reserved for it on whatever computer will be holding that website. This could be the computer owned by the Internet Service Provider although as even the smallest database will probably take up more space than that offered free by the Service Provider the price will have to be negotiated.

Should that prove to be too expensive the website could always be hosted by some third party as mentioned previously.

Alternatively the company might decide to dedicate one of its own computers to the job and link that to the Service Provider which would be the expensive option. Here not only would the cost of a dedicated computer have to be taken into account, but so too would be the cost of any support personnel needed to keep the computer operating on a twenty-four hour basis.

To make matters worse the benefit of a website such as this could be measured only in terms of improved service rather than reduced costs. Even so in a highly competitive world who can afford not to give the best possible service?

Product Information

Where some companies have a complicated product range a website could be the perfect medium for guiding customers to the right choice for them. An obvious example here would be the financial services industry where all manner of personal questions have to be asked before an individual can be given a suitable pension plan. In fact any situation where choices have to be made which, in turn, lead to further choices could be suitable for this type of website. The programming would be obviously more complex than for a simple advertising website, but not too much more. The only real problem would be designing the structure of the site rather than programming it.

From a management point of view the issue to be addressed is cost as a site like this could work out to be very expensive. It would only make sense to help customers make the right product choice if, at the end of the process, they could then order it on-line. This means the company would have to run its own servers (computers) with all the equipment and personnel costs that entails. The sheer volume of new customer information generated by the website would see to that. It would have to, the site would only be viable if a large amount of business was done over the Internet.

Anything less and the value of that new business, or rather the profit made from it, would never be enough to pay the site costs. In cases like this the only question is, will the website produce sufficient business? A good website can help to maximise what business there is, but beyond that fine tuning the only people who can answer that question all work for the company paying the bills.

Process Information

There are some industries where customers might need, or want, to know the exact status of an order currently going through the system of some supplier. An obvious, and well advertised, example of this is the freight industry where a haulier's website can be used to show the current position of any package being carried by that company. Simply by entering a unique customer or job number the route, shipping and despatch details can be made immediately available together with an estimated delivery time.

For anyone needing to know such information (like expeditors, stock controllers and factory managers) the benefits to them are obvious, which is another way of saying that the company who owns the website can offer an improved level of service.

Obviously this applies to more than just the transport industry. There are many other companies who could be capable of offering the same service which is now known as B2B or Business-to-Business commerce. The sole requirement is having customers who regularly need to know the status of a particular order as it progresses through the system. In essence, then, it is suitable for any company that can afford it.

As to that the costs are difficult to determine even on a very generalised basis. Fairly obviously the first requirement is that the information is available in a computerised format. If not then probably the best solution would be a brand new computer system with Internet access built in. Even if that is not necessary the costs would have to include linking the entire corporate information system to the Internet which could only be calculated on an individual basis depending entirely on how easily the two could be integrated - but expect it to be expensive.

On the other side of the coin if a supplier has introduced, or is planning to introduce, this type of service then being able to make use of it could be seen as an additional advantage to any of its customers who might be considering using the Internet.

Related Information

A good example of this could be a manufacturer of winter sports equipment offering   up-to-the-minute information about skiing conditions as a part of its website. The idea being that potential customers would use that site for its information value and in the process become exposed to the company brand name and product range. In other words a pure marketing exercise which could enhance the status of that company within the industry and raise its prestige amongst potential buyers. To what extent this status and prestige could be translated into extra sales is a question only the Marketing Department could answer, but undoubtedly some good would come of it.

Even so the site itself would be expensive to maintain simply because the information would have to be continually updated with all the administrative problems that would bring. In different industries a different type of information could be offered which was less subject to change, but the underlying problem would still be there. Not only that, but the cost of obtaining this information in the first place also has to be considered.

It is possible for a company website to also act as a chat forum. In Internet-speak a chat forum is a site where individuals can leave text messages or even have on-line text-based "conversations" with other people using the service at the same time.

There are, in fact, a great many of these already in existence each one dealing with a particular topic, but the massive diversity of the Internet means there is always room for one more. An example here would be a trade organisation setting up a website where its members could express their views on issues concerning them all (like new government legislation for example).

It would be just as easy for a company to include a chat forum on a specific subject as part of its website although the benefits would be harder to quantify.

So, as can be seen, an information website can be many things. It could even be several different things put together. All it takes is the imagination to find the need and the money to fill it. Alternatively, of course, it could be none of the above and yet still be a valuable company asset (or a drain on its resources).

Trade

The real strength of the Internet lies in the fact that it is a two-way medium of mass communication. Unlike television, radio or the print media a website offers an inter-active content which can, under certain conditions, make it ideal for trade. Imagine a stand at a trade fair where every visitor is interested in the product on offer and came specifically to buy and that is what doing business on the Internet can be like, with the added bonus that this particular trade fair never closes. In a competitive world who could ask for more?

Yet people who set up businesses on the Internet frequently do ask for more. Specifically they ask for more sales because the sad fact is that the amount of business done over the Internet is nowhere near as great as the hype would have it. In a lot of cases people will simply not buy off a website (not enough to make the venture profitable anyway.)

From the experience gained by companies already operating in this market place it is apparent that the only companies who can expect to do well are those who operate at the low price, high volume end of their particular market, either that or they sell very specific products. For example things like books, videos, music and CD-ROM's can all be successfully sold over the Internet because the product is a known quantity no matter who is the seller. (Any copy of a best-seller book is the same as any other and the video of a Hollywood movie will always be a video of a Hollywood movie no matter where it is bought.) Even so the companies doing well on the Internet usually have a well-established trade name in more conventional retail outlets. As Internet analysts have now discovered a well-known brand name is even more important on the Internet than it is on the high street.

Needless to say the size of the profit margin on the goods being sold by a particular company will also have a bearing so it would be wrong to totally disregard the option of a sales website. Instead, if anything, it should be considered as a long-term investment; something that is unlikely to yield an instant profit, but which in time could grow to be a valuable source of revenue. Until its customers have sufficient confidence in the company to start placing repeat orders and word of mouth brings in new customers the short-term losses will just have to be accepted.

Even so there are other points to consider, all of which stem directly from the fact that anyone who opens a website is selling to the world. This raises two fundamental points: transport costs and customs regulations.

Selling to the World

It may seem obvious, but sending a parcel to the other side of town is not the same as sending it half way across the world. Yet if sales come via the Internet the customer could well be on the other side of the planet. All of which means that whenever Postal and Packing costs are quoted on a website they will have to be on some form of sliding scale depending on the exact whereabouts of the customer. If not the company could lose more money on transport than it gains by doing the business in the first place. (And not quoting delivery charges might deter potential customers as they would then have no idea what the total cost would be.)

Secondly, many countries have special requirements when it comes to the import of goods. For example Australia demands that all wood products be specially treated to guard against fungal growth - and insists on seeing proof of this before allowing them into the country. Given that here wood products does not just mean items made of wood, but the packing case they came in that could significantly add to the costs which anyone would do well to bear in mind.

Also remember that some goods being sent abroad as part of a commercial transaction need to be accompanied by the appropriate customs docu-mentation, even when being sent through the post to a private citizen. There is nothing particularly difficult about filling these forms in, and they are freely available from the Post Office, but doing it takes time. Someone has to devote part of their day to doing the paperwork which is an added cost that has to be paid for out of the profits of the website.

Obviously companies who already export their goods will have these systems in place, but the point is any company who operates a website is a potential exporter and should know these things before they begin.

Those who forget could find that doing business over the Internet is a very expensive option indeed. Even without that a sales website will be expensive to set up. Quite apart from the programming involved in the web pages themselves the site will have to be integrated into the company ordering system which could cost even more.

And that on top of the fact that the company may have to use its own computers to host the site with all the added expense that involves. In other words it is not for the faint hearted.

To be fair there are many companies now moving into the business of providing complete web commerce solutions which includes everything from the software needed to run a sales website to its hosting and security. Of course, while these packages can much simplify the process they cannot guarantee sales. In fairness, though, they can make it much easier to set up a web commerce operation and the packages should be investigated for that reason alone.

So, while it is possible to make money from a website, and many companies do, that is by no means the end of the story. On the Internet it is possible to make money even from websites not specifically geared towards trade.

How? Read on.

Advertising

By selling space on their own website to advertisers many companies can at least offset the costs of their on-line operation and in some cases even make a profit on the deal. As the principle, and the prices, are by now well established this is something every company should consider.

There are, in fact, two main ways for a company to sell space on its website: Banner Advertising and Click-Through.

Banner Advertising

Banner Advertising is simply an advert on a screen. Whenever someone visits that website then, alongside whatever it was they visited that website for, they will also see an advert similar in concept to those used in roadside hoardings. Normally this is charged on the basis of cost per thousand impressions (visitors) otherwise known as CPM. How much a company can charge for this obviously depends on all the usual factors that make up the cost of advertising such as how many people will see the advert and their income group.

Click-Through

Click-Through is where a visitor clicks on a particular area of a web page and is immediately taken to another, completely different, website. Usually that particular area of a web page is an advert in its own right which, not unsurprisingly, includes the words 'Click Here'. This kind of service, which can deliver visitors genuinely interested in the product being advertised, can obviously command a higher price than the simple banner advert.

In either case the advertising revenue gained can be enough to make any website a viable proposition and for that reason alone should be seriously considered. Even so it would still be a good idea to contact an on-line media planning agency, of which there are many, for an accurate forecast of any possible income. After that the entire business of going on-line can be treated like any other project: consider what is wanted, consider what is feasible, perform a cost-benefit analysis and take a decision.

It may well be that the company decides the Internet is not for them, and some well known companies have come to exactly the same conclusion. Alternatively the company might want to go on-line immediately, but, whatever way it goes, at least let the decision be based on knowledge and solid business principles. When company money is being spent that must be a firmer basis than hype and misinformation.

Summary of Points Worth Considering:

♦ Can the company survive without a website? Will it lose business to on-line competitors?

♦ Is the product being offered suitable for e-commerce? In some cases customers prefer to feel and touch before buying.

♦ Will the customer base be expanded? If so by how much and what effect will that have on profitability?

- Will a website take trade away from existing outlets? If so what will the consequences be?

- Could it reduce support costs? If so by how much?

- Could the Internet help to find alternative suppliers?

- Are there problems communicating with smaller sub-offices or overseas agents?

- Would access to more information make the company more efficient?

- Does the product need to be supported? Can a website replace help lines and would that reduce company costs?

- Will it help customers choose the right product? Is the product range so complex that customers need to be guided through it?

- Does the customer need to know the status of an order being processed?

- Are there procedures in place to export goods? If not how much will it cost to establish these procedures?

- Could advertising space be sold?

Chapter Two

Going On-Line

Deciding the ground rules for any new venture will help you to clarify what it is you want to achieve, in the short and long term. When a company decides to go on-line there are two things it should never do: the first is give the job to the IT Department and the second is give it to sales. This is because the IT Department will treat it as just one more job to add to the list, and anyway IT departments traditionally have little or no knowledge of any long term company plans. Sales, on the other hand, will more than likely see it as an excuse to put all the company promotional literature onto the Internet. Neither way will produce a decent website.

The Internet is a brand new medium and should be treated as such. That means give the job to someone who has the vision to appreciate just what can be achieved and sufficient knowledge of future company objectives so that the website can be a part of them. Technical expertise can come from people co-opted to the project, or brought in especially, but the overall flair - the feeling for the job - must be there from the start if only to keep the Internet project going in the right direction.

That said the serious business of planning to go on-line should now be considered. A process complicated by the fact that different websites call for different levels of planning. In which case perhaps the best idea would be to first cover the basics which all potential website owners will need to know and then move on to areas specific to a particular type of website or company operation. That way this chapter can at least claim to be logical.

Perhaps it goes without saying, but under normal circumstances the first step would be to decide what type of website is needed. However, if the sole reason for working through the procedure is to produce some form of cost-benefit analysis then choosing a website might not be so easy. It could even be the case that a type of website will be chosen purely on the basis of cost, once that has been established. If so decide what type of websites are likely to be wanted and do separate costings for each.

Similarly as the second step is to allocate a budget that too can be skipped, at least until the other costs can be determined. All of which means that the best place to start is at step three: choosing a name.

Choosing a Name

Whenever a company, or individual, goes on-line they are allowed to choose the name their websites will be known by. This is the part that begins WWW, and which can now be seen in practically every advert, although it should properly be referred to as a URL or Uniform Resource Locator. Away from such jargon what this really means is that the company, or individual, now has a unique name which can be mapped to the Domain Name System (DNS). As will be explained later in Appendix B this is so any other computer on the Internet can connect to that website once its name, or URL, has been entered into whatever Browser that computer happens to be using. It is, therefore, reasonably fundamental to the entire process.

Using an ISP

It also has its own pitfalls to trap the unwary and so as much care needs to be taken here as with any other aspect of going on-line. To begin with it is possible to include the name of the Internet Service Provider which would give something like AOL.COM/COMPANYNAME or COMPUSERVE. COM/PRODUCT. (Technically speaking this means that the company website is part of the Service Provider's domain.) While this may be the easiest method, and more than adequate for an individual, no-one could say it looked professional. Not only that, but if for any reason the company decides to change its Service Provider it will also have to change its URL (web address) which is likely to be printed on all its stationery.

Using a Domain Name

To avoid that the answer is to register the company as a domain in its own right which, in fact, means thinking up a website name and then telling the relevant Internet authorities what it is and where it can be found. In theory this can be done by the company itself, but in practice it is usually better to let the Service Provider do it. The cost will be slightly more, but the Service Provider's greater experience in these matters will make a mistake less likely. Even if the service provider adds an administrative charge on to the cost of registration the whole process will still only be what might best be described as pocket money prices. For those who prefer the hands-on approach the process is not too difficult as all it really involves doing is entering a chosen name into a particular type of website which will then search the entire Internet to see if that URL (web name) is already in use. If the name has already been taken either think of another name or try and buy the existing name from whoever owns it. The process really is that simple and it can be done by entering "domain name registration" into any of the Internet search engines. (For more on search engines see later.) This will then provide a list of websites any one of which will search the Internet for URL's.

Next comes the question of which domain the company wants to be a part of. This is where it starts to get complicated. Although something like COMPANYNAME is a domain in its own right so that, for example, COMPANYNAME/SALES is part of the same domain and needs no further registration the company domain must also be part of a larger domain which specifies what type of organisation it is. This is where the rest of the name comes from and explains the .co.uk or .com endings which all web names have.

Whenever a computer tries to find a particular URL it begins by searching, for example, the UK domain which tells it where to find the .co domain so that this can be searched for the website name. In technical terms each domain is said to be below the domain listed to its immediate right in any address. For example if the full web address was WWW.SALES.COMPANYNAME.CO.UK then the SALES domain is below the COMPANYNAME domain which, in turn, is below .CO the way that particular domain is below .UK. It does make sense although it might need thinking about for a moment or two. Then it has to be decided which domain the company will be registered under.

Standard Naming Conventions

In fact there are several to choose from, each for different types of organisation. In the UK they are:

.co.uk   Commercial organisations
.org.uk   Non-profit organisations

.sch.uk	Schools
.ac.uk	Academic institutions
.plc.uk	Public limited companies (Rarely used)
.ltd.uk	Private limited companies (Rarely used)
.net	Organisations running a large network

Fairly obviously the .uk ending denotes a UK company and would naturally be different if the company was based elsewhere. (For example .jp is Japan, .nl is the Netherlands and .fra is France.) Also just as obviously only public limited companies can use the .plc.uk. domain the same way only private limited companies can use .ltd.uk. although either could use .co.uk if they preferred. Even so .co.uk is very much the industry norm with .plc.uk and .ltd.uk being rarely used.

For companies who would rather not reveal their national origins there are some international domains which they could just as easily register with. These are:

.com	Commercial organisations
.org	Non-profit organisations
.edu	Educational establishments

On the Internet, being a member of an international domain is often taken to mean being American, certainly the Americans themselves seem to think so. That is why all their commercial websites use the .com domain when, properly speaking, they should be .co.us. This can be useful as some companies report that transatlantic business is better when people believe they are buying from a company based in the US. Other than that the only advice is to choose a name which is in some way associated with the company. HEYDUDE.COM might sound like a good way of catching the youth market. But if the company is called Smith and Jones Ltd it would take an extensive advertising campaign before that particular strategy paid off.

Better by far is to stick with a name that can be easily guessed so the website can be found that much easier. A good example here is the BBC having as one of its websites the name BEEB.COM although this was in many ways a case of making a virtue out of a necessity. BBC.COM is in fact owned by a company called Boston Business Computers (and the first page of its website includes the comment 'This is not the BBC On-Line').

Of course whatever the name chosen the decision is entirely up to the company. The sole criteria is that no-one else has already registered it which can be a problem in itself - and one that has already resulted in legal action.

The Law

When it comes to the registration of names the rule is: first come, first served. In practice this means that if two companies both wanted to register the same name then, as every name must be unique, only one of them could do it - and that would be the first one to apply. No matter what the respective sizes of the two organisations the name would be allocated on that basis alone. For example if a firm of candlestick makers called Ford wanted to register their name on the Internet, and if no-one else had registered it first, then they would have a perfectly legitimate right to use that name for their website regardless of a certain motor manufacturer. Of course, big business being what it is, the two could come to a private arrangement which the system does allow for, but unless or until that happens the Internet rules would be on the side of the candlestick maker.

The more cynical will by now have realised that a rule like that is heaven-sent for those interested only in making a fast buck and, indeed, the courts have been asked to make a judgement on this more than once. The first was in January 1997 when the Harrods department store went to court to secure ownership of the name HARRODS.COM which had been registered by another, totally unrelated, company. On this occasion the judge ruled that as Harrods was a recognised trade mark only it could own the domain of that name.

Later in the same year a prosecution was brought against a company called One in a Million Ltd who had registered a whole range of names. Although the company claimed there were all for personal use their defence fell apart when evidence was presented which proved they had tried to sell the name BURGERKING.CO.UK to the Burger King chain - for a mere £25,000 plus VAT.(Approximately $45,000.) As the company had also registered, amongst others, the names SPICEGIRLS.NET, MACDONALDS.COM and BUCKINGHAM-PALACE.ORG the judge decided these were not names likely to be readily associated with that particular company and ordered them to cease the practice. From this several points arise:

◆ Protection is not guaranteed. In the examples quoted all the companies concerned operated on a global basis and very likely had their company name and trademarks registered world wide. It was this which gave them their real protection, not the law. As no other company could exist with the same name it was easy to claim that the relevant websites should be owned by those same companies. Even so no definitive law has been established so any other enterprise which wanted control of a website domain registered in its name would still have to go through the courts. Yet without such international status to fall back on the chances of a legal victory are a lot less clear cut. It could even be that another organisation with the same name exists in another part of the world and is trading perfectly legitimately over the Internet. As proof consider the fact that in Britain ASDA means a chain of supermarkets, but in the United States it means American Student Dental Association. (Both organisations can be found on the Internet.)

◆ Names should be registered. Even if a company has no intention of joining the Internet it should still register all its trade and brand names as Internet domains. If not they could be registered by anyone from a competitor trying to steal business to those who could put the website to a lot more mischievous use. (A process now referred to as cybersquatting.) In either case the company would suffer and the only recourse would be a very expensive law suit which they may or may not win.

◆ All domains should be registered. If a company registers, for example, the .ltd.uk domain that would still leave the .co.uk and the .com domains free for others to register. Again this would only be to the long term harm of the company concerned so, as trade and brand names are valuable assets, protect them by registering them.

As an example of what can happen the NASA website is, unsurprisingly, NASA.ORG which signifies it is a non-profit making organisation. (Anyone wanting the latest news of the space shuttle or pictures sent back to Earth by deep space probes should look here.) Unfortunately NASA forgot to register any other domains which explains why the NASA.COM website offers pornography. Exactly how much the owners earn from the site is unknown, but the chances are high that they collect an incredible amount of passing trade from people entering the wrong name into their Browsers. From this comes the moral of the story: while NASA might be big enough, and famous enough, to rise above all of this how many other organisations could survive being implicated with a website containing pornographic or other offensive material?

For the sake of completeness it should also be mentioned that many people recommend using only the company name as the Uniform Resource Locator or URL (which, for those who have forgotten, is the correct term for a domain name). The idea here is that anyone can then just enter the name of a particular company into their Browser, take a guess about whether it is in the .com or .co.uk domain, and still find the website. In fact the latest Browsers automatically search the other relevant domains if the first choice produces no match which shows the principle to be sound if nothing else. It also vastly simplifies the choice of a name, but if a different choice has to be made for some reason no lasting harm will be done. So-called search engines exist which are designed to find all the websites matching specified criteria. For a commercial website that is more than sufficient.

Finally, remember that spaces are not allowed within a name. Should that name consist of more than one word the convention is to run them both together so that, for example, Smith's Car Hire would become Smithscarhire. Again by convention hyphens between words are not used although as the Sunday Times does it lesser companies are unlikely to come to too much harm.

In short, choose a name, or even a collection of letters, that works and if it happens to be unallocated then use it. The sole restriction is that the international domains (.com etc) should be no more than 22 letters and national domains (.co.uk for example) must be no more than 80 letters. After all, there are a lot more things in life to worry about than choosing a domain name, and a lot more to consider when planning to go on-line.

Choosing an ISP Provider

Choosing an ISP (Internet Service Provider) is no different from choosing any other supplier - and the same care must be taken. Obviously cost is an important factor, but, as with any other supplier, the type of service being offered together with the quality of that service are just as important. The only difference is that, where the Internet is involved, managers are often moving into unknown territory. Because of this the only place to start any discussion on ISPs is with that initial contact when a company first decides it wants to go on-line.

First Contact

Any ISP is likely to offer potential new subscribers a demonstration of exactly what it has to offer. Sometimes this can take the form of a CD-ROM which, when played, can simulate the on-line experience - or so the claim goes. In fact running software straight from a CD-ROM is nothing like using the Internet. For one thing a CD-ROM drive can transfer data to a computer many times faster than a modem, making it impossible to judge the speed at which the Internet works. (The slowest CD-ROM drive transfers data at slightly more than 300,000 Bits per Second, BPS, rising to over 3.6 million BPS for the latest drives. By contrast the fastest modem transfers data at just 55,600 BPS, and that only under perfect conditions which very rarely exist.)

Secondly any sample web pages on that CD-ROM will have been designed for whatever Browser technology is also included. This means they will be state of the art wonders full of moving pictures, exotic graphics and a wide variety of special effects which are only possible when no-one has to worry about making their website compatible with all Browsers, all versions of that Browser, and the availability, or otherwise, of any plug-ins. The real world is not like that.

Lastly no CD-ROM can truly simulate the effect of surfing the web (jumping from one website to another). This is because on the Internet jumping/surfing to another website involves searching for the address of that website through the Domain Names System, connecting to it via what could be several different computers and finally downloading the website itself. All of which takes time. However, on a CD-ROM where none of this is needed the connection is practically instantaneous. In short that CD-ROM might be interesting to watch, but anyone who thinks it represents real life is in for a huge disappointment.

Alternatively the ISP might offer a more practical demonstration either by having a sales team visit the company with the system already set up on a laptop computer (which these days have modems built in) or by hosting some form of seminar in the function suite of a local hotel. In either case there are points to be aware of which even the reputable companies neglect to mention.

Checkpoints in a Demonstration

◆   First, and most obvious, is the fact that any demonstration of Internet activity will be carried out using the fastest possible modem. At present this means a data transfer rate of 55,600 Bits Per Second (BPS) which is fine for anyone intending to access the Internet using a similar modem, but not so good for anyone who wants their website to be viewed by others. As these other visitors are likely to be using modems capable of no more than 33,600 BPS, or even 28,800 BPS, the time scales involved in downloading a web page should be adjusted accordingly.

◆   **Ensure the Demonstration is 'Live'.**
Next comes the issue of those web pages which will be displayed during the course of the demonstration. While there is no doubt that these will be genuine web pages it is highly unlikely that they were pulled straight from the Internet while everyone watched. To explain, all Browsers have the ability to automatically store the contents of web pages on the hard disk of the computer running the Browser (to use the technical term they are cached to the hard drive). This is done so if anyone wants to return to a web page previously visited it can be read from the hard disk which is considerably faster than taking it from the Internet for a second time. Of course while this might save time, which it does, anybody not knowing those web pages were already cached to the hard drive could easily mistake their speed of retrieval for the speed of the Internet when the two are vastly different. To counter this the best method is to enter the address of a website not already stored on the hard disk. As all Browsers have a menu option marked 'HISTORY' clicking on that will show a list of all websites visited, and therefore cached, so a URL (web address) not shown can then be entered. A good choice for this is the website which nowadays all Hollywood movies have as they are well advertised and, more importantly, tend to be full of complex graphics. In this way not only will the full flavour of the Internet be experienced, but the time taken to download the website will be valuable experience for anyone about to argue with a web design agency who will doubtless want to create something similar.

◆   **Timing the Demonstration.**
Next, if at all possible make sure the demonstration takes place in the middle of the afternoon never first thing in the morning. The point of this is to take account of what is sometimes referred to as the America effect. Basically when the USA starts work in the morning so many people log onto the Internet that the entire system becomes congested and slows down to a noticeable extent. For this reason everyone on the European side of the Atlantic is always advised to do their web surfing in the morning when the time difference means America is still asleep. On the other hand, as potential newcomers to the Internet should see it working under average operating conditions before they buy in to it, demonstrations should be held in the afternoon when the whole of America is on-line. That way everyone can know for sure what they are getting before contracts are signed and money is spent.

Linx

Some ISPs will advertise their membership of something called LINX which, they claim, is the sign of their professional status. In fact LINX is the London Internet Network Exchange, an interconnection point for British ISPs. (To be accurate beyond the ISPs are the Network Providers who own the physical side of the Internet such as the telephone lines and all the electronics the system depends on. It is these various networks which are connected together by LINX.)

Fairly obviously as LINX is a purely British operation any call made by a British company to a British website will be faster if the ISP routes its traffic through LINX which is why some ISPs make that claim. However, as Internet traffic between Britain and America is slightly slower through LINX not every ISP uses it. Instead they have their own line to the USA which results in faster transatlantic traffic, but slower access to UK websites. The difference is measured in seconds either way so the only real question is whether a particular company intends to use just British websites, in which case LINX is the best bet, or will it more likely use websites in other parts of the world. For those who intend to do both the phrase swings and roundabouts is appropriate, certainly without a good solid reason to base their decision on no company should choose an ISP solely because of its membership, or not, of LINX. There are, after all, far more important points to be considered; such as:

How Much Web Space is Offered?

All ISPs offer a certain amount of space on their computer where corporate, or personal, web pages can be stored. Exactly how much space is offered differs between the various ISPs, but, even then, the real question is, how much space will a particular website need - and if more is needed than is being offered how much will the extra cost.

What Software is Being Offered?

Some ISPs offer their own Browsers and email software as part of the price while others just include a variety of shareware packages. (Under the shareware system software is given free for an evaluation period of typically thirty days. After that it must either be paid for in full or removed from the computer.) Although any software offered will do the job, if the ISP produced it themselves any upgrades are likely to be free which is not the case with shareware. There not only will the upgrades have to be paid for, but so will the initial cost of the software which will be on top of any price quoted by the ISP for using its service.

Additionally if there are problems with using the software an ISP will probably have a help line for its own products while with shareware the individual manufacturers would have to be contacted - assuming they had a help line and assuming they were based in this country.

It has to be said some shareware packages can easily be as good as more commercially produced software, there is nothing inherently wrong with using it, but if that is all the ISP has to offer it should be reflected in the price.

On a related issue there is no contractual reason to stay with the software supplied either by the ISP or, in the case of Windows 98, as part of the basic system. As there are now many types of software available, each with their own good and bad points and each calling for different amounts of memory or processing power try experimenting with a few to see which one is best suited to the organisation. In all cases the software is either given away free (like Microsoft Internet Explorer or Netscape Navigator) or, alternatively, payment is deferred until the company adopts it as the software of choice so no cost is involved.

If the company decides to follow what is known as the Internet cafe route where an Internet connection is established in a rest area to reduce the novelty factor before going entirely on-line this would also present a perfect opportunity to experiment with different types of software. (For reasons why an Internet cafe might be created see the section on plans and policies.)   As the computer being used would have no connection with the company network there would be no security issues involved, nor would it matter how much duplicate software was stored on that computer. Furthermore if the final choice of which software to use was left to the people most likely to use it this would have the effect of making them feel more involved in the project. In systems development terms they would 'own' the system which means they would be quicker to adopt it and less resistant to the changes which would necessarily be involved.

How Many email Addresses are Being Offered?

Similarly all ISPs offer a certain number of email addresses (known as aliases) although, again, the exact number differs between the various service providers. As with web space this raises the question of how many are actually needed and how much will any extra cost.

Will there be Bandwidth Limits or Charges?

If a website is 100k (meaning it holds 100 thousand bytes of information) and the ISP has imposed a limit of 100mb (100 million bytes) per month then simple arithmetic shows that the website could only be sent out over the Internet 1,000 times a month. To take this further, as a website is sent out over the Internet every time it is visited (which is how visitors see it on their computer) then that website is limited to just 1,000 visitors a month. This is known as a bandwidth limit.

Some ISPs impose these limits to prevent one subscriber from taking too much of the available capacity and, consequently, leaving less for others. As an alternative some ISPs impose an extra charge once the number of bytes sent exceeds a pre-defined limit, but, in either case, this is something that should be known from the outset.

How much of a problem this is can only be calculated on an individual basis once the size of the website and any bandwidth limits are known so very little advice can be given other than to do the sums. Then take a warning.

If an ISP offers no bandwidth limit to all of its subscribers how can it prevent its link to the Internet from becoming so congested that no-one can get through? A question well worth the asking.

What Visitor Information Can Be Provided?

All ISPs should be able to provide a wide range of information about the people who visit a particular website. At the very least they should be able to tell the number of visitors together with where in the world these visitors come from and whether one web page was accessed more than others. Such information is vital. For example if the website shows an email address, or if visitors can request more information from the company concerned simply by clicking on that option in the website which automatically generates an email message to the company, then only by knowing the number of visitors can the effectiveness of the website be judged. If a large number of visitors produces only a small number of emails there is obviously something wrong with the site.

On this subject the difference between a visitor and what is known as a hit should be known. Whenever a particular computer file is accessed, i.e. read, by a Browser a hit is recorded which is where the confusion comes from because a web page will typically have several files which collectively make up that page. By way of explanation think of a newspaper front page which could have one banner headline, five stories and two pictures. That headline, those stories and those pictures would all be produced separately and then brought together so the page could be printed.

In other words eight separate items were brought together to make up that one page. Apply this principle to web pages and, in the above example, eight files would have to be opened before the web page was complete. So just one visitor would equate to eight hits. All of a sudden the difference becomes important to anyone trying to collect statistics about their website.

How Will the Service be Charged?

When it comes to using, or surfing, the Internet all ISPs will offer at least two different billing methods: a flat fee per month, or year, which gives unlimited access to the Internet at no extra charge or a simplified pay per use scheme, usually charged by the minute. Under the latter option subscribers will be charged a certain amount for every complete hour they are connected to the Internet in addition to their subscription fee. Perhaps obviously under the first scheme the one-off payment means no further charges will be made no matter how long anybody uses the service.

As with any other choice offered by any other supplier there will be a break even point, in this case when paying by the hour is no more or no less expensive than paying a flat fee. If the expected Internet usage is less than this then, it goes without saying, paying by the hour is the best option, but that must be very carefully monitored. Internet use within a company can easily increase without anyone being aware of the implications - until the bills arrive. At this point it is worth mentioning the growing number of ISPs who offer Internet access for free, paying for the service by advertising and taking a percentage of the call charges from the telecoms provider. For home use this is a perfectly adequate service, but anyone planning to use the Internet for business purposes would be well advised to pay a subscription charge. The problem here is that by offering free Internet access the ISPs concerned have to operate on wafer thin profit margins that leave very little room for equipment maintenance or upgrades. In the natural course of events this inevitably means a lack of reliability in the service which can be tolerated by a home user, but not a business.

Considering that if a website is unavailable for even a single day the company could lose more than the entire annual subscription, no matter how much that may be, free Internet access has to be seen as a false economy. Better by far to pay for Internet access as that way service levels can be asked for and guaranteed.

Are Round the Clock Repair Facilities Available?

As the Internet is a twenty-four hour a day operation it therefore follows that any website must be available for that same twenty-four hours a day.

This is only possible if the ISP can immediately repair any faults, or cure any problems, that may develop in the normal course of their operations. Fairly obviously this means a repair team must be on constant standby, either that or accept having no Internet access for what could be extended periods. (If repairs are only carried out during normal office hours a problem could develop one night, be not even looked at until the next morning and could then take all day to repair. In the Internet that is a long time by itself and it could be even longer if the repairs have not been completed by the end of the working day.

Is the ISP a Content Provider?

Some ISPs offer nothing more than access to the Internet while, in addition to plain Internet access, others offer what is known as content which actually means a range of information and services available only to those who subscribe to their service. Examples here would be stock quotes, weather forecasts and technical or professional information. Needless to say subscribers will be charged more for this whether or not they use the facility, but it would be wrong to dismiss these content providers out of hand purely on the basis of cost alone. If a company needs up to the minute information on a particular subject it may well be that this is the cheapest method of acquiring it.

Alternatively the fact that a company now has access to such information, perhaps for the first time, could be seen as an added benefit to using the Internet.

What is the Ratio of Subscribers to Modems?

ISPs only have a certain number of modems which have to be shared between all subscribers so it is important to know the ratio of one to the other. Given that if every modem is being used no-one else can access the service until one of these modems becomes free this is obviously an important question for anyone who expects an instant connection to the Internet.

The generally accepted figure is no more than ten subscribers per modem although even here there could be problems if there was a peak in demand at any time during the day.

For this reason it is a good idea to ask the ISP what their policy is on this matter. They might have a lower ratio than 10:1 when a company first subscribes to their service, but if new subscribers are then taken on without extra modems being added that ratio could soon rise to unacceptable levels.

Will Commercial and Private Subscribers Use The Same System?

If an ISP is trying to sell its services to the home as well as the corporate market this could cause problems for the business user. While this might not be apparent during normal office hours anyone working late could easily find the system swamped by other subscribers using it for recreation. It may even be that the same problems are experienced during the day when schools are on holiday. Properly speaking if an ISP wants to be in both markets it should be oper-ating separate systems for each. That means separate telephone numbers and a separate set of modems. Anything else could mean businesses being denied the service they would still have to pay for.

What Support Is Available?

From time to time every user will need help with their Internet connection. There will always be a need for someone to answer questions which typically begin with, "Why can't I..." or "How can I..." and for this reason every ISP should have a telephone support line staffed by people who can answer those questions. Where the ISPs differ is in the times those support lines are open. With some this will be strictly office hours while others offer a more extensive service. Needless to say when help lines are the issue the sole criteria to base any judgement on is, will they be available when needed. For companies who work to office hours themselves the help lines need only be available then, but if anybody expects to work late then so too should the help lines. If not support will be denied just when it is needed the most.

What Precautions are there Against Power Failure?

It is a strange fact, but ISPs seem particularly prone to power failure. (It was for this reason that Judge Zobel's ruling in the case of English nanny

Louise Woodward who had been found guilty of murder, which was intended to be broadcast over the Internet first, had instead to be made public by more conventional means. A circuit breaker failed just one minute before the announcement was due.) Even if that power failure occurs in the middle of the night and is soon repaired it would still be a problem for anyone wanting to use that service the following morning due to the twenty-four hour nature of the Internet. With information constantly passing through those computers any failure causes a log jam which can only be slowly cleared when power returns; sometimes this can affect the service for days.

How Often Are Backups Made?

Installed on the computers of the ISP will be all manner of software, including websites belonging to its subscribers. As such not only must the ISP have backup copies of all this software, the backups must be sufficiently recent to incorporate the latest changes to every one of those websites. In other words backup copies should be taken on a daily basis (the way it happens in every other business!).

If an ISP has a problem with its computers, which every company does from time to time, then usually the easiest solution is to wipe all the files from the computer and restore everything from backup. As this is almost recommended practice it therefore follows that those backup copies must be kept up to date at all times because no-one can predict when a problem will occur. Anything else means a company website, if restored from backup, could be showing everything from an out of date price list to special promotions no longer being offered - all of which will upset its customers.

For a company to keep its own backup copy of its website is also a very good idea, but that does not remove the responsibility from the ISP.

How Good Is Security?

A great deal of company information is likely to pass through the service provider's computers. In some cases it might even be stored there, perhaps over an entire weekend, until the company next logs on to the Internet. Because of this the security procedures followed by that ISP have just got to be good.

In this context security also means more than just safeguarding whatever password each individual subscriber uses to gain access to the Internet via the service provider. Nowadays so-called sniffer programs exist which can be secretly installed onto the ISP's servers (computers) to sniff out confidential information and pass it on to whoever installed the program in the first place. Usually these sniffer programs search each message for particular key words, like 'Confidential' or 'Financial' for example, which trigger it into action although it will do the same should any password be found, including those owned by the company itself. (Perhaps to let outside callers, from a different branch office for example, gain access to their internal computer system.) If that happens a data thief could then use that password to gain access to the company's own computers with untold consequences.

For this reason the ISP must carry out regular security sweeps of every piece of software installed on its computers to find and eliminate these programs before they do any damage. Failure to do this could mean that a cheap Internet connection turns into the most expensive purchase that company ever made.

Will The ISP Screen email for Viruses?

An increasing problem for companies is the number of computer viruses that can be attached to emails. (Strictly speaking they are attached to such things as word processor or spreadsheet files which are sent via email, but the principle remains the same.) To counter this some ISPs now offer to screen all incoming emails to prevent any viruses reaching their subscribers' computers. While this is obviously useful the service, needless to say, has to be paid for. Even so making full use of it is still a very wise precaution.

On a related point the fact that an ISP screens for viruses in no way reduces the need for a company to do its own virus checks on any emails. Because of the highly destructive nature of some modern viruses a belt and braces approach is the only safe policy.

The good news is that practically every ISP should be able to answer these questions, and those that do not should be ignored. Even so as the answers they give will all vary, those differences by themselves will help to point the way towards making the right choice. Better yet, since these are in no way complicated or overly technical questions, they should help to bring the choice down to price, service and quality which any other supplier would have to face. After which move on to other matters, like drawing up a plan for going on-line.

Planning Issues

As must by now be obvious there is a lot more to the business of going on-line than just buying a modem. In fact a whole range of issues have to be addressed, most of which should be done before any money is spent or contracts signed. Like any other project a website needs careful preparation and like any other project there should be clearly defined steps along the way so progress can be measured.

Fortunately these steps, or milestones, require very little in the way of technical expertise nor are they particularly difficult, but in the long term it would pay any company to follow them.

They are:

Set Objectives
◆   What will a website do for the company?
◆   How will visitors be attracted to the site?
◆   What will make them return?
◆   What are the business objectives, advertising or trade?
◆   How will the return on investment be measured, just in financial terms or will less tangible factors be taken into account?
◆   Can the investment be cost-effective?

Develop a Policy
◆   How will the website fit in with other marketing or corporate plans?
◆   Who should be involved in the project to keep it in line with other plans?
◆   What effect will a website or Internet connection have on current working practices and what will any changes involve?
◆   Will the website be developed further in the future?

Agree the Content
◆   What information will the website contain?
◆   Is it available?
◆   How often will it need to be updated?

- How will it be organised on the website, by region, demographics, or some other way?
- What else will the website contain and how will that be organised?

Settle the Technical Issues
- Where will the website be hosted?
- What other sites will it have links to?
- What other sites will have links to it?
- Will extra telephone lines be needed, should they be leased?
- Will existing hardware or software need to be updated?
- Will staff need to be trained?
- Has a security policy been decided?

Settle the Financial Issues
- How much will a website cost to create?
- How much will it cost to maintain?
- If staff training is needed how much will that cost?
- How much will any future website development cost?

A company which takes the time to answer these questions can be sure of having a firm consensus about what it hopes to achieve and how any results can be measured. Even so there is still more work to be done.

Policy Issues

Before any company starts using the Internet there are certain procedures which it must have in place and enshrined in company policy. This is not so much because the Internet offers new ways of working, which it does, but because failure to do this could result in anything from massive financial penalties to legal action being taken against the company concerned. That might seem like scare tactics, but in this case it happens to be the literal truth. The first of these concerns staff browsing the Internet.

Browsing the Internet

Any company with an Internet connection will find its staff browsing the Internet for websites that are in no way related to work. This could be done during a lunch break, and with the full blessing of the management, and yet even then the company could find itself facing prosecution.

The problem here is pornography. It might not be as prevalent on the Internet as the tabloids claim, but it is still there - and very easily found. All it takes is a simple search and even the most inexperienced web surfer could soon find links to thousands of different sex sites. In other words if staff are allowed to browse the Internet expect pornography to be downloaded from day one.

While that might not sound like a major issue remember, the law makes no distinction between pictures on a wall and pictures on a screen. That means the company could find itself facing charges of sexual harassment or constructive dismissal every bit as easily as if they had allowed a pin-up calendar to be openly displayed. In some cases just having those images stored on company computers could be enough.

Against this there can only be one line of defence: make the downloading of any such material a disciplinary offence - and strictly enforce it. If staff want to surf the Internet in their own time, and if the management allow it, there are plenty of interesting, amazing and downright bizarre websites to be found without looking for pornography. There should be no need for it and it should not be allowed, not when it puts the company at risk.

And on that note, there are other websites to worry about. In this case Hackers websites.

Hackers Websites

These are websites full of information about how to defeat computer security systems and view confidential information. There are even some sites where specialist software to do exactly that can be downloaded. This gives rise to two problems: if staff try and if they succeed. To take those in reverse order, if anyone succeeds in viewing confidential material the consequences should be obvious although perhaps not quite so obvious is the fact that, under the Data Protection Act, it could lead to prosecution in extreme cases. (Under the terms of the act failing to adequately protect confidential information stored on a computer is in itself a criminal offence.)

Yet even worse could be the consequences of a failed attempt. If some inexperienced user tries to change system settings, tamper with access control procedures or launch highly dubious software just because they heard about it on the Internet the results could be catastrophic. Without properly understanding what they were doing that user could bring down the entire corporate computer system - and when a system crashes for that reason it could be a long time before it could be restored to full working order.

For that reason alone a company policy on Internet surfing and file downloads has to be implemented before going online and it must be backed up by the strictest possible disciplinary measures. Companies who hold a great deal of confidential information or who cannot survive without computer support should also seriously think about regularly inspecting the hard drives of all their computers for unauthorised software. That might be hard to sell to their staff, tact and diplomacy would have to be used, but the security of the company must be paramount. If need be the problems associated with pornography could be cited as further justification. Failing that mention the other problems associated with downloading software (for which see the chapter on Security).

Despite its apparently trivial nature there are serious risks involved in this kind of web surfing and the only sensible course of action is to eliminate them before going on-line. Afterwards might be too late.

Productivity

Similarly there is one aspect of going on-line which no Internet evangelist would ever admit to: immediately afterwards productivity will fall sharply. In part this will be because learning to use the new, on-line, system will take time although the major reason will be pure curiosity. Staff will surf the web far more than is necessary just to see what is out there. One way to avoid, or at least reduce, this is to install some form of monitoring software which can restrict access to certain specified websites or, alternatively, creates a list of all websites visited which can then be inspected by a senior manager. Fairly obviously staff would have to be notified in advance if any such software was to be installed, but, other than that, there should be relatively few problems. (Even so be aware that this software does not work well enough to restrict access to all pornographic or objectionable websites. It should be used together with a firm company policy not instead of one.) An interesting alternative is to establish some form of Internet cafe, perhaps in a staff rest area or restaurant. If this is done before the company as a whole goes on-line then when it happens the novelty factor will have worn off and people will be more inclined to use the Internet as the business tool it is supposed to be.

email

Next comes the policy on email which must also be firmly established - and just as firmly enforced. Once again this is an area where a company could run into problems. In this case for several reasons, most of which have to do with the nature of email itself. In normal face to face contact the actual words being spoken account for only a small percentage of the commun-ication taking place. Body language, facial expression and tone of voice all combine to determine how these words are interpreted. For example, des-cribing someone as a lunatic could be a strict statement of fact, a term of endearment or an insult; the listener would decide which based on the visual clues offered by the speaker. With email there are no visual clues. All the recipient has is printed words on a screen which means the potential for misunderstanding is tremendous. Although there are ways to reduce the risk (for which see the chapter on using the Internet) it will never disappear entir-ely and managers should be aware of this, and of the possible consequences.

First amongst these is the fact that the informal nature of email can easily trap someone into making a comment which might be perfectly acceptable in a face to face meeting, but which could be grossly insulting, or even defamatory, when those words appear on a computer screen. Also remember that a name on an email gives no clues as to the gender of the person sending or receiving it nor, in an increasingly multi-racial society, to their ethnic background. For example a comment made in an email to J. Smith might be taken as a joke by John Smith, but would Jane Smith see it in the same light. An important fact of business life which must be considered. Just as importantly, if an email comes from a company address there is very often no clear way for anyone receiving it to distinguish between a personal opinion and official company policy.

For this reason a strict policy should be in place which explicitly bans all racist, sexist, obscene or defamatory comments. It should also ban any mention of competitors or rivals. That last point may seem strange, but even emails meant for internal consumption only, i.e. within the company, can still form the basis of court action and marking them as

'Private' or 'Confidential' is no defence against libel. In which case how much more likely is it that litigation will follow if defamatory emails are sent outside the company. In other words make sure all staff members know what the company policy on emails is and, just as importantly, make sure they know why.

In a highly competitive world no-one should risk the kind of dubious reputation which a careless email or two could develop. Far less should they risk alienating a customer the same way, not when all it takes to prevent it is a simple warning to every member of staff. If need be this can be backed up by the use of monitoring software which allows some designated staff member to read every single email sent out through the company system although, legally speaking, this can be a potential minefield.

Privacy Issues

To begin with every employee has what is known as an expectation of privacy which means they have the right to conduct private conversations, or send private emails, without their employer eavesdropping. Therefore, they must be told in advance, and it must be agreed in advance, if any such monitoring software is to be introduced. In the eyes of some legal experts this eliminates any expectation of privacy although this has yet to be tested in the courts so this is not so much a case as the jury being still out on the subject. In a very real sense the jury has not even been sworn in.

Similarly any union representative should have the right to use the email system for union activity without having that monitored by the employer. Not only that but any employee should have the right to communicate with their union representative through the email system also without having that monitored by the employer. On a practical basis this can probably best be solved by having a separate email account (address) reserved for union business although as this would still be susceptible to monitoring the real issue is the amount of trust placed in whoever actually reads these company emails.

As yet this is not covered by any law, but it is imaginable that some employer somewhere would abuse the system which in itself would very likely lead to legislation being introduced, not to mention a great deal of industrial unrest.

For that reason the best idea is to establish the policy right from the beginning and be sure everyone knows why it is necessary. By being open about the problem it can be expected that both staff and unions will behave reasonably and accept the need for restrictions.

Alternatively if less draconian measures are acceptable, it might be worth considering a so-called sig file. Short for signature a sig is a few words added to the bottom of an email. Usually these are some form of joke or humorous sign-off, but they could just as easily be a disclaimer to the effect that any comments made are personal and do not reflect company policy. As most email packages include a facility to add these sigs literally at the click of a mouse, once they have been created naturally, there is very little reason for not using them - and a tremendous incentive for doing it. (It may sound like a cynical reflection on modern day life, but the only people who are sued are those who can afford to pay out significant damages. An individual employee is unlikely to be sued, instead the lawyers will always go after the company where the email originated from.)

Legal Issues

Then comes the question of legality. Potentially this could be even more important because the courts are very reluctant to accept emails as evidence. They can be forged too easily. To put that another way. If a company accepted a contract, or changes to a contract, by email alone then unless they follow the correct procedure they would have no legally acceptable way of proving that contract or email even existed should a dispute arise.

For this reason companies must develop the habit of printing out copies of any important emails. Until the courts decide what non-paper evidence is acceptable to them forget all thoughts about the paperless office and print those emails out. Furthermore they must be printed as soon as they are received then signed and dated by two, preferably three, people. The printed copy should then be locked away safely. If this is done then the testimony of the people who signed it, confirming that it was received on that specified date from that specified company, plus the document itself will form the basis for a valid legal defence. As the people who signed it will likely be employees and therefore subject to undue pressure as regards their testimony the defence will not be watertight, but for most disputes between trading partners it should be enough.

For companies who want to go beyond that the only solution is to instigate a policy where financial or contractual documents will only be accepted by email on the basis that a more conventional written document will also be sent within an agreed space of time. In this way the speed of email can be married to the legal enforceability of the written document to produce a highly efficient and highly secure service.

To complete the picture a company must also have a firm security policy in place, but, as any precautions would only make sense when the dangers are understood, this is dealt with in the chapter on security.

As can be seen, then, planning to go on-line involves a lot more than simply deciding to join the so-called information superhighway. In fact it is very probably the failure to give enough consideration to the planning stage which causes some organisations to come to grief when they do in fact start using the Internet. This is understandable. With so many companies now being pressurised to use the Internet the temptation must be strong to skimp on the planning, always assuming these companies know there is any planning to be done.

A secondary problem is usually the lack of decent advice. That being the case take as much advice as is offered, from this book and elsewhere. Much of it will be contradictory so always ask for the reasons behind each statement to separate vested interests and personal opinions from facts then decide if it all makes sense. If not think very carefully before joining the Internet. As the saying goes, never play a game for money until you know the rules.

With the Internet the rules are not all that complicated, but they should be well known before any money is spent.

Summary of points worth considering:

◆ Does the person in charge of the web project know enough about future company objectives to include the website in the overall company strategy?

◆ What name will be chosen?

◆ What domain will be used?

◆ Choose an ISP

◆ Set objectives

◆ Develop a policy both for website development and for email, downloads, pornography and web surfing

◆ Agree the content

◆ Settle the financial issues

◆ Settle the technical issues

Chapter Three

Web Pages

Your web page is your company's face on the Internet, but web pages, like beauty, are all in the eye of the beholder. Where one will see a boring website full of nothing but text against a coloured background another will see a well organised, highly informative, website reeking of professionalism.

Equally where one will see a state of the art, excitingly original, website another will see nothing but needlessly flashy graphics and far too many special effects. Opinions will always vary.

Timing Your Launch

For this reason one idea worth considering is to delay creating the company website until after the Internet connection is in place. That way the people who will be ultimately responsible for the presentation of that website can take some time to surf the Internet and see for themselves what is possible and, just as importantly, what they like. Needless to say any web designers they hire will have totally different ideas, but at least the argument can begin from a position of knowledge on both sides which has got to be better than putting blind faith in the judgement of an outsider.

Frequency of Changes

On that subject there is another point anyone interested in creating a website should be aware of, concerning the frequency of design changes. Any book, magazine article or web design agency will always insist that a website should be frequently updated, in some cases on a week by week basis. The argument goes that unless a website is re-designed on a regular basis visitors will get bored with it and stop coming which, despite what the designers might say, is true for only a small number of sites.

This is another example of conflicting agendas. The magazines cater mainly for the so-called recreational surfers, those who do it for fun, and so any advice given to website owners is slanted in this way. As such the advice given is perfectly accurate, people who visit a website for entertainment expect to be constantly entertained by something new or else they look elsewhere, but none of this applies to the business community. There a site can remain unchanged for years with no loss of trade because the people visiting it expect information not entertainment. For as long as the price list or product details are current that website is more than acceptable.

Obviously there will come a time when it has a dated look, like any other advert or promotional literature, but until that day arrives no-one should be under any compulsion to change it no matter what a design agency might say. Especially not when that agency has its own reasons for wanting clients to change their websites on a regular basis. (They get paid for the work involved.)

Know What You Want

That said now is the time to consider the delights of web page design. Again this is more involved than might be supposed although, fortunately, the subject can be broken down into distinct categories. These are: choosing a design agency, web page design, promoting a website and legal considerations. While it might at first appear contradictory to have a section on choosing a design agency and then another on web page design as any agency should know how to design a website there are sound reasons for this.

By knowing the basics of what constitutes a good web page, and what points to be careful of, any manager will be in a much stronger position when it comes to detailed discussions with the agency of choice. That way no-one will ask for the impossible, nor will anyone be able to offer sub-standard work.

Even so there is one golden rule which must be followed before design agencies are even approached and that is know what the website will be used for. Have meetings, circulate memos, collect opinions; do whatever it takes, but always be in the position where an agency can be approached to create a website which will perform a stated function. If this rule is ignored not only will the agency have a too vague brief to work to, which can never produce good results, but if that website then fails to produce the results expected the company will only have itself to blame. On the other hand once a company knows what it wants it can then start looking for an agency who can do it.

Choosing a Design Agency

Here the first point to keep in mind is that, in this industry, there is no such thing as a one man business or, to put that another way, no one person is capable of creating a decent website alone. There are just too many skills involved for any individual to master them all. Consider, a website needs graphics artists to design everything from the colour scheme and choice of typefaces to the positioning of any pictures and corporate logos. It also needs programmers to convert these designs into something a computer can accept by using whatever software or plug-ins has been previously agreed. (To understand plug-ins see Appendix C: Web Software.) Finally it should also have someone in overall control of the project both to resolve any conflicts and to make sure the designs stay true to the stated aim of the website. As all of this is too much to expect from one person the best, or some would say the only, solution is to make web design a team effort - and then find an agency with the right team.

Fortunately this is made easier by the fact that the work of any web design agency is highly visible, on the Internet. All it takes is to ask the design agency for a list of their previous clients so those particular websites can be inspected as a means of assessing the work of that agency. In the trade these are known as reference sites.

It all sounds perfectly straightforward, but be warned there are some sites where authorship is claimed by more than one agency so whenever a client list is given check with the clients first; make sure the agency did create the sites it is now offering as evidence of past work. After that there are several other points to keep in mind:

Compare Like with Like

If a website is wanted purely to advertise the company name it is pointless to look at websites which do more. Similarly if a website is wanted that must be capable of performing many functions there is nothing to be gained from looking at advertising websites. Only those websites which perform a similar function to the one the company wants to commission are worth looking at because only they can show how well a particular design agency can do the job in question.

Ask the Right Questions

To get the best results from looking at these reference websites, and to compare the work of one agency with another, it helps to look at each web-site with a clear purpose in mind. The easiest way of doing this is to prepare a series of questions to be asked of each site visited.

Typically this would be:

◆ How fast did it download? If a site takes too long to appear on computer screens the average user will just move on to the next site without bothering to wait.

◆ How easy was it to navigate? If anyone has problems moving from page to page they are more likely to give up and move on to the next site rather than stay and try to work out what they have to do.

◆ How well presented was the information? No matter how good a site looks if the information it contains is presented in a confusing style no-one will bother coming back.

◆ Did the graphics add or detract from the presentation? Were the pictures and charts an aid to greater understanding or were they just there for show.

◆ Did all the reference sites look the same? If all the reference sites looked similar it usually means the design agency has taken an off the peg, one size fits all, approach. This could still be perfectly acceptable, but if so the minimal development time should be reflected in the price being quoted.

◆ How well did it do the job asked of it?

◆ What was especially good about it?

◆ What was especially bad about it?

◆ Did it create the right corporate image?

◆ Did it feel right?

Although questions like did it feel right or did it create the right corporate image are highly subjective nevertheless they should still be asked. An agency which produces work that a company feels to be right is more likely to create a website the company will be happy with.

Will the Same Team be Used?

An agency might have more than one design team and while they might be happy to show the work of their best team there is no guarantee that these same people will be creating your company website, or at least not for the quoted price. This is especially important where some or all of the design team are freelance workers hired for an individual project, but who may no longer be available. It, therefore, pays to ask the question.

Ask More Than One Agency

When all of this is done there will very likely be more than one design agency still in the running, each one of which should be approached. (As a slight digression do not be put off by those agencies which style themselves as cyber-architects or some other piece of pseudery. Designers are trendy by nature so this sort of thing has just got to be lived with.) The best way to open the negotiations with any agency is to submit a design brief sometimes known as a Request For Proposal or RFP. This should be no more than a one page document and should cover such points as: what the site will do, who it will target and what its character will be like i.e. will it be formal, informal, jokey, text only or full of graphics.

As this will form the basis of any work done by the agency it would be a good idea to first circulate it to all relevant people in the company commissioning the project for their approval. Nothing delays work more, or increases costs faster, than a change to the specifications when the job is already half completed.

If need be the same document could also specify what technology is to be used although a case can be made for letting the agency decide that once it knows what type of site is needed. However, if this latter option is followed always ask how much experience the agency has with whatever hardware or software is being proposed. (For the reasons why see the appendix on web software.)

Be Realistic

Also, be realistic. No website, no matter how good, can revolutionise a company's business; nor is it likely to be an overnight success. These things takes time so start off with down to earth expectations and hope to be pleasantly surprised. In a lot of cases the arguments between company and design agency is caused not by any shortcomings in web design, but by the company having overblown expectations as to what a website can achieve. Try to avoid this if only for the sake of maintaining good relations with a new and important supplier.

Equally so, being realistic means be prepared to pay a reasonable price for decent work. An agency might offer a seemingly unbeatable cut-price deal, but like every other such deal it usually means a cut-price service. Some agencies quote on the basis of a price per page which admittedly has its advantages, the total cost is known in advance, but it can also have its drawbacks. Sometimes the agency can be tempted into cutting corners to reduce development time and so increase profits. For the same reason if an agency offers a fixed price per site deal the first question they should be asked is how many hours worth of work would be involved. If the answer equates to an exorbitant rate per hour there is room for negotiation at the very least.

On the other hand if the agency cannot answer immediately take it as a sign that the job has not been thoroughly costed and assume the worst. Any company who accepts a job without knowing how much it will cost them either has a massive profit margin built in to the price or else they are riding for a fall. Also keep in mind that any price quoted should cover the three basic elements of website creation which are: design, maintenance and hosting.

Design

This is probably self-explanatory. The design element is the creative part of actually producing a website.

Maintenance

This involves such things like making sure the links to other sites still work, updating any information or making cosmetic changes to the site. As such it is drudge work of the kind creative designers hate so make sure regular site maintenance is included in the contract and also make sure the frequency of this maintenance work is specified. Regular could be defined as once a week or once a year, it would be as well to know which.

Hosting

Once the site has been designed it then has to be stored, or hosted, on a computer somewhere before it can be viewed by the other Internet users. Needless to say unless it is hosted by the company who paid for the site a fee will be involved which should be known before any contracts are signed. Sometimes the agencies have financial or other business links with companies who host websites which could represent a conflict of interest when hosting decisions have to be taken. Be certain that when an agency gives any advice it is done for the benefit of the customer, you, and not themselves.

It may well be that an apparently good deal being offered by an agency covers only the design element, with maintenance and hosting fees on top, which is why the question should be asked and the costs clearly itemised. Similarly it is possible for an Internet Service Provider to offer web design as part of its overall Internet package, but here too the costs should be split. More importantly there should be separate contracts for each. That way if a company wants to change its service provider it can still retain the design agency. Alternatively, if a company wants to use a different design agency it will not have to find another service provider at the same time.

Also, while on the subject of changing design agencies, be careful about who owns the copyright for any work done - and have it put in writing. If this is not done and the agency retains the copyright by default then the only way to change the design team would be to commission a brand new website, or buy the copyright off the original agency which would likely work out expensive either way. It is also worth remembering that in this context copyright should apply to more than just any pictures or charts used. To be worth having it must equally include what are known as the scripts which means the back end programming that makes the website function.

Checking the Final Product

Finally, keep everything in the real world. Once an agency reaches the point where it has a website to demonstrate make sure that demonstration takes place over the Internet and is not read straight off a computer hard drive at a speed no modem could ever match. It is also a good idea to try reading this website using more than one Browser (say Microsoft Internet Explorer and Netscape Navigator). That way the company paying the bills can see how fast, or otherwise, their newly created website can be downloaded and what other problems it might cause for the different Browsers. It also means that if there are problems or the download takes too long they can make the agency do something about it before they get paid. (Before this demonstration takes place remember to check the History option on the Browser. If the website has already been accessed it will be stored, cached, on the computer hard drive and its name displayed in the history listing. Delete this and the test will be honest.) If all of this is understood from the beginning, and put in writing, that should be enough to concentrate the minds of the agency's design team.

Another very good idea is to use a Browser known as Amaya which is supp-lied by the W3 Consortium and can be found at WWW.W3.ORG/Amaya. This can best be described as a test Browser in that it will only read web pages that conform to standards laid down by the W3 Consortium. If Amaya can read it any Browser can read it. Letting the design agency know their work will have to pass this test is an excellent way of keeping them in check. Then all that has to be worried about is the actual design of those web pages.

Web Page Design

Frames

One of the first issues likely to be raised by any web design agency is the subject of Frames. A good place to start is with an explanation of exactly what Frames are.

Any software which runs under Microsoft Windows will always have a slider bar at the extreme right of the screen. The idea being that if more information is available than can comfortably fit onto the screen then clicking on the slider control causes that information to slide, or scroll, up the screen and into view.

This, in principle, is a Frame. The only difference as far as web pages are concerned is that the screen, or page, could be split up into several areas, known as a Frame, each with their own slider control capable of bringing different information into view. In this way the use of Frames can make a tremendous amount of information available on a single web page - always assuming the Browser being used can actually read Frames. Not all do which is a problem in itself. Some websites offer two versions of each web page, one for Browsers that are frame enabled and one for those that are not which does solve the problem, but only by massively increasing the complexity of the website design. Not to mention increasing the cost by an estimated 25%. Away from that the problem remains.

This is probably something that can only be answered on an individual basis. In which case take advice from the web designers (not all of them are cowboys), consider the alternatives and take an informed decision. Nothing else can be said.

International Standards

Unfortunately there is still a lot more to say on the subject of web page design, but before going any deeper into that subject two general points should be made, both of which concern the fact that the Internet is a global medium. Firstly be careful about the format of any dates mentioned. For example the date 3/12/2001 will be read as either the third of December 2001 or the twelfth of March depending entirely on what part of the world it is read in. Therefore make sure the date is shown in a less ambiguous way, something like 5 Jan 2001, so there can be no confusion. In exactly the same way if a time is mentioned for any reason the time zone being used should also be specified. 9.00 AM GMT is a lot different from 9.00 AM EST, but unless visitors are explicitly told which it is they will have no way of knowing when some advertised event is about to happen.

Content

As to creating a website, that comes down to one simple rule: content. Also known as information this must be the core of any web project as it is this which people want when they visit a particular site. Clever graphics or fancy design work have their place, but unless there is a reason to visit that site, and keep coming back to it, everything else is just a waste of time and money.

For any company about to commission a website this means its content (information) must be decided in advance and delivered to the design agency before they start to do any work. Leaving it until later, or hoping that the content can be added once the site has been designed, can only lead to confusion, delays and a very badly organised website. Should anyone think otherwise then remember that the sole point of any design work is to illustrate the information. Design, no matter how good it is, can never be an end in itself. If that is accepted then the point about content becomes clear because without knowing what information is to be presented how can any design agency do its job? (As a slight digression this also helps to show how important the planning stage is.)

What follows, then, assumes the content is in place and that only design factors have to be considered. Even so that still leaves a lot of issues to be resolved, of which the first few can be settled without going anywhere near a computer. This concerns what is sometimes described as the site architecture which really means how each individual web page connects to the others and how easy is it to move between them. Properly speaking this should be done at the paper stage, when the site design exists only on paper, as if it is done later any changes would be that much harder to make. Here the points to watch out for are:

◆ **Is it Logical?**
   The information should flow in a logical manner from one page to another in a way that makes sense to the average user so that navigating the website (moving from one page to another) is practically self-explanatory.

◆ **Is it Well Structured?**
   Every page should have a link to any and every page that might be

next required and these pages must have a link back to the previous page. In addition every page should have a link to the home page. (The home page is the one that first appears when a website is visited. Typically it would have a company name and some kind of menu system allowing visitors to go directly to whatever information or service was being offered.)

◆ Is it Simple?

An overly complicated website will deter visitors the way an unhelpful sales assistant will stop them using a particular shop. If visitors, or customers, cannot immediately find what they are looking for and no help is given they will look elsewhere.

◆ Is it Complete?

The entire site should be checked carefully to make sure that every link is in place and that every page has a link to it. In other words first check the links to confirm they go to the right page and then check each page to make sure it does actually have a link. As an example of what can go wrong there is a website in existence (which had better remain nameless) where the company who owns it offers a free monthly newsletter, to be sent by email, covering various technical matters relevant to the particular market it operates in. As a way of keeping the company name in the mind of potential customers this is an obviously good idea (and its website advertises the newsletter on every single page). Unfortunately they forgot to check the links so the one place no one can reach is the page where visitors register their email address to receive the newsletter. The fault might lie with the web design agency, but it is the company being made to look foolish.

It is also at the paper design stage where some of the more technical matters should be resolved. The first of these is to confirm that the site will not be what is sometimes referred to as Browser-specific which means making sure that the site can be read by all Browsers and all versions of that Browser. There are all manner of enhancements available which can produce extra special effects on a website, but which cannot be handled by all Browsers. As a consequence of this using these extra add-ons restricts the number of people able to view the site and, therefore, limits the number of potential customers who will see it. Know what is involved before any software enhancements are used.

Secondly make sure the screen resolution will be as low as possible. High-resolution photographs might look good, but unless the site is advertising a photographic studio no one will care too much. What they will care about is the fact that high-resolution pictures take longer to download.

Actual Design

After that comes the actual design of the site which is, in many ways, difficult to write about. While there is a great deal of advice that can be given much of it would apply equally to any document or design project and, as such, is outside the scope of a chapter specifically devoted to web page design. Because of this there will be no advice such as not using too many different typefaces or any other general design tips. Instead this section will concentrate only on those issues which are exclusive to web pages.

Of these the first, and by far the most important, is: remember the Internet is a different medium.

A company brochure could have a picture of the factory on the front page, or some other picture chosen to illustrate the advertising slogan splashed across it, with pictures of the entire board of directors spread throughout the inside pages. It could also have pictures of the sales team or possibly even the entire work force which might make for a good brochure, but it would make an abysmal website. The difference is that a brochure is given away free and can be read by people at their leisure while with a website someone has to pay for the on-line time and then sit and wait for totally irrelevant pictures to appear on the screen in front of them. None of which will make them think kindly about the company who owns that website.

At the risk of appearing cynical the only people who might want to see pictures of board members on a website is the directors themselves and if a design agency offers this look on it as straightforward ego pandering - and refuse to accept it.

To soften the blow slightly there are also many other differences between a brochure and a web page and many more points to consider. These are:

Make Something Happen Immediately

A large graphic (picture) at the top of the page means a visitor will have to stare at a blank screen until it finally appears. Just as likely they will hit the STOP button on their Browser and move on to another site so give them something to do while they are waiting. That means have a fast loading piece of text at the top of the screen, something like "Welcome to the website of...." will do, or anything else as long as it holds a visitor's attention. According to researchers the average time spent by web surfers on an individual site is just eight seconds; unless something happens within that time to make them stay they will have moved on.

Remember Cultural or Historical Differences

The Internet is a global medium accessed by people from a wide variety of cultural or ethnic backgrounds. Unless that is kept constantly in mind the scope for causing distress or deep offence is tremendous. An obvious example here is images of women on a website. This does not necessarily mean the stereotypical picture of a scantily clad model draped over a sports car or anything remotely like that. What it means is that in some parts of the world any image of a woman is forbidden by religious law. It may seem strange to western eyes, but in other countries it can be a major part of their culture and should be respected - especially if anyone wants to do business with that country.

Likewise other countries also have a different history and different sensibilities which should equally be considered. Comments about Agincourt or Waterloo are unlikely to win too many contracts from France.

Remember the Language Barrier

English might be the most popular language on the Internet, but not everyone speaks it as their first language. It is, therefore, a good idea to keep any text as simple as possible to cater for these people who might otherwise have difficulty in understanding the words used. One idea often found on websites is to put various national flags on the home page so that visitors can click on whichever flag is appropriate to them and see the text in their own language. It might make the website harder to design, but such consideration could score points when contracts are being awarded.

Keep it Short

Web pages are a very visual medium. In practice this means that unless visitors are there to read a specific piece of text, like a reprint of a magazine article, a screen full of text will put them off. To prevent this make liberal use of headlines and bullet points to make the information more easily digestible. Sometimes on the web less can be more.

Keep it Visible

Sometimes an important piece of information can be at the very bottom of the page and therefore not immediately displayed on the screen. Although the slider control could be used to bring the rest of that page into view in practice this is not always done and the bottom of the page stays unread. As a result either important information will go unnoticed or, where that information includes a link to other pages, the site will be practically impossible to navigate. To counter this a good idea is to put the links close to the top of the page where they can be easily seen and also make it obvious that there is more to the page than appears on the screen.

Promoting the Website

Once the website is operational the next step is to let everyone know it exists, and then somehow persuade them to come and pay it a visit. This is in fact two slightly separate problems. Just telling the world that your site exists is no guarantee they will want to come and see it. (Everyone knows where Antarctica is, but few people want to go there for recreation.) That being the case it would be best to start with publicising the website; attracting visitors to it can come later.

Tell Everyone Your URL

The standard advice given to any company at this point is to make sure its URL (web address) is displayed on all their letterheads and adverts. Although that might seem obvious there are still traps to avoid, not the least of which is only do this after the website is launched; never before. There are those who say the site should be advertised practically as soon as its name has been registered, but that could lead to disappointed customers. If anyone tries to visit that newly-advertised website and finds it not there (because it has yet to be created) they are unlikely to go back for a second look no matter how well the site is publicised.

Similarly, wait until the site has been completed before inviting the public to come and see it. Nothing looks worse, or more unprofessional, than a site full of under construction notices. (By convention if a link leads to a web page not yet created a message should appear which says, quite literally, 'Under Construction'.)

Use Search Engines

Also, while on the subject of web page construction, a lot can be done here to make the site more visible to the Internet using community. So-called Search Engines exist which are, in reality, complex pieces of software designed to compile huge lists of every single website on the Internet and then index them according to certain key words. The idea being that anybody who wants to search the Internet simply enters a key word into the search engine and it then returns a list of all the websites matching that particular key word. (For a further explanation see Appendix D.) The point of all this is that the people who own the website get to decide what key words their site will be indexed under. Within HTML itself there is a command known as <META> which allows for either 1024 characters or 200 words to be placed between the two <META> tags. These words will not appear on the web page as seen by any visitor to that site. Instead they will be seen only by the search engine which will use them to index the site under those words. As this, in turn, determines whether or not a particular website will be listed when somebody uses that search engine to find a specific reference it follows that these key words must be chosen with care.

Therefore:

◆ **Take the decision in-house.**
   A design agency will not necessarily know the best words to use. As these words are meant to attract the target market they should be chosen only by people who understand that market.

◆ **Think of the searcher.**
   What words would a searcher by likely to use? They are the words that should be included.

◆ **Use slang or jargon if necessary.**
If a general slang or industry-accepted jargon term is available that too could be used.

◆ **Be accurate.**
Any word must be relevant to the site in question. If not, with an ever increasing number of websites to index, the companies who own the search engines might refuse to accept a particular URL. For example if a company sells car accessories then the word PORSCHE would be acceptable only if it was a recognised dealer in Porsche merchandising. Using the word just to attract anyone interested in cars would be against the rules.

◆ **Do not be too specific.**
Try and include a few words of a more generalised nature. In the example above the company might not have been able to use the word Porsche, but it could still use such terms as 'sports car' or 'fuel economy'. That way the net is spread just a little bit wider to bring in extra customers (always assuming it did supply devices for sports cars or fuel economy).

There is every possibility that those 200 words, or 1024 characters, which at first appeared to be so much will rapidly become not enough to do justice to the site. Unfortunately 200 words is the limit so a certain amount of horse trading will have to be done. That may turn the process into more of an art than a science, but nothing else can be done. The rules, as they say, are the rules.

Also keep in mind that not every search engine is prepared to seek out new sites; some expect the owners of these new sites to register with them, typically by means of a form on their website. This might be an optional service offered by the design agency, but if any extra charges are mentioned just remember the registration process is free. And just to add to the workload there are also other ways of making people aware of a website - like a carefully chosen link strategy.

Link Strategy

Although there is no law, or no ruling, about websites providing links to others it is still a good idea, and for more than one reason. Firstly when search engines provide a listing of all sites matching a particular criteria they give a higher priority to those sites which have links to others. In practice this means a company website will be closer to the top of the list and so more likely to be selected. Considering that searches against some categories can produce lists of several hundred thousand websites anything which brings one particular URL closer to the top has just got to be a good idea. Secondly, of course, it can be a good way of attracting visitors.

In fact there are some sites which include a page full of nothing else but links to other sites covering a particular topic in its widest possible sense. These are the sites which tend to get Bookmarked. (The Browser is told to store that particular web address so it can be returned to again and again at the press of a button. In Microsoft Explorer it is known as a favourite.) This way not only does a company website get constantly re-visited, but that page holding the links would be prime advertising space.

So having the right links can be highly beneficial. The more so as it is usually a two way process; links to a particular website should be accompanied by a corresponding link from that site. In which case the only question left is how can these links be arranged in the first place.

Here the most obvious thing to do is get in touch with owners of other sites and offer a swap. Both sites provide a link to each other. These other websites could be providing a complimentary product, their market could be demographically similar or it could be any other site where a case could be made. As every single link has the potential to bring fresh visitors to the site there is no such thing as having too many.

On that basis another good way of attracting visitors to a website is to advertise it on the Internet itself using so-called Banner Adverts.

Banner Adverts

As the name implies these are adverts which take the form of a banner across a web page except, unlike other adverts, some of these incorporate a link so that clicking anywhere on the banner takes the visitor directly to the site being advertised. As such they can be highly effective although, as with any other advert, first of all the location has to be right.

One highly recommended place to advertise is on the web pages of the various search engines as these are the places everyone is guaranteed to visit at some time or another. Not only that, but as these search engines rely exclusively on advertising to pay their costs, and to make a profit for their owners, any one of them will be more than happy to discuss terms. Usually two options are available. The first is to sponsor a particular word or phrase so that whenever this is used by anyone searching the Internet the advert appears on the results page. (The list of websites matching the search criteria.) Alternatively there is RoS or Run of Site where the advert appears every time the search engine is used although, naturally, this comes only at a price.

Other than that any website could be suitable, assuming it already attracts the market being aimed for. Here the main point to consider is quantity difference. If both sites are likely to attract approximately the same number of visitors a straightforward swap arrangement would be the most appropriate. However, if one site is likely to attract significantly more visitors than another a paid-for advert is the only solution for reasons which should be obvious. As to how these sites can be found the answer is easy: search the Internet. Use a search engine, enter a word or phrase any member of the target audience might enter and the resulting list of URLs are all candidates as places to advertise the company website.

In other words finding somewhere to place the advert is easy, making people take notice of it is an entirely separate problem. Fortunately there are various techniques to improve the response rate, but before they are discussed a word of warning about the way statistics are misused on this issue.

The standard response rate for any banner advert is 2% which sits oddly with the claim that a certain technique can improve throughput by 15% or more. In fact what it really means is that throughput, or response rate, will be increased by 15% of 2%. For example if 1000 people visit a particular site just 20 (2%) can be expected to take notice of a banner advert. Should some method be employed to increase this by 15% what it actually means is an extra 15% of 20, i.e. 3, making a total of 23 in all. While a response rate of 23 per 1000 is obviously better than 20 per 1000 it is still a lot less than the 150+ per 1000 which might have been expected although few agencies bother to explain it that way.What follows then is a variety of accepted methods used to increase response rate, but always bear in mind that the percentages quoted translate into a lot less visitors than might be hoped for.

◆ **Use Animations**
As this is eye-catching it can increase response rate by 25%.

◆ **Use Cryptic Messages**
Curiosity alone can increase the response rate by 20% but as no-one knows what kind of site they are about to visit not all of the extra visitors will be the right kind of audience.

◆ **UseStatements**
Comments like 'Click Here' or 'This way to....' can increase the response by 15%.

Similarly bright, eye-catching, colours or free offers can also increase the response although the exact amount would depend on what was being offered for free. It is also a good idea to have two or three different adverts, each one placed on a separate website. That way, by analysing where visitors come from, it becomes possible to judge which advert is the most effective.

PR for the Site

Finally, there are some agencies who recommend that launching a company website should be a high profile promotional event. In some cases this might even be true, but before going too far down that road find out if the design agency has any trade or financial ties to a PR or advertising agency. Their advice could still be valid although it hurts no-one to have this sort of thing out in the open. There are now PR agencies whose brief is to solely promote your site on the Internet and in the press.

After that start considering the legal implications of owning a website.

Legal Implications

Despite media reports to the contrary the Internet is not a law-free zone. In fact the opposite is true. Being a global medium anyone publishing on the Internet is theoretically subject to the laws of every country in the world. Although the implications of that are dealt with further in the Appendix on Government and the Law there are, nevertheless, some issues which come a lot closer to home. Of these the first, and the most perfect example of the problems caused by world wide cyber trading, concerns the matter of exclusive licences.

How Exclusive is Exclusive?

There are many companies selling products for which they have been granted an exclusive licence, but only for a specified geographical area. Outside of that area some other company would have the licence to sell the product which is where the problem comes from because the Internet knows no geographical boundaries. This means from the moment that product appears on a web page the company owning that website could be in breach of its licensing agreement - and every other company in the world trying to sell that same product would insist on action being taken, if only to protect their own market.

While this might not seem like much of a problem to those companies without exclusive licenses to worry about there is a similar situation with regard to copyright which should be of concern to everyone. Once again the issue is the global nature of the Internet. In this case while a company might have permission to use copyrighted material, in its sales brochure for example, that permission might not extend to the entire world. It could well be that any such permission was granted only for a particular country, meaning if that material was used on a web page it would be an infringement of copyright.

To go on from there. Any company is likely to have its own material on its website over which it wants to retain control; it owns the intellectual copyright. Yet if this was published on such an easily accessible, global, medium as the Internet it would stand very little chance of enforcing that copyright unless its website specifically stated that such copyright existed. For this a solicitor should be consulted over the exact wording.

Even then a company could find itself facing litigation over the content of its website, or the links from it. However, as that is two separate issues they should be treated separately. To begin with web content. In a highly litigious age every company should take steps to protect itself which, in practice, means including a legal disclaimer in its website.

Disclaimers

Although no amount of legal disclaimers will save a company from prosecution if information on its website caused damage to property, personal injury or death nevertheless their use is still highly recommended. All it takes is a statement to the effect that visitors using any information on that website do so entirely at their own risk. Needless to say it could be dressed up to say that every effort is made to ensure the accuracy of that information, but even without that a disclaimer can provide a great deal of protection. After all, not even the biggest company could keep track of every piece of legislation in every country in the world, but just one change, anywhere, could invalidate the information on a website, for that country at least. And if that happened the company could find itself apparently recommending an illegal act for which it could be prosecuted unless its disclaimer was worded carefully.

Even when the cost of legal advice is added to the equation a disclaimer can still save so much for so little cost that not to include one makes no sense at all. In fact the only real argument should be where on that website will it be placed.

A solicitor would argue that the disclaimer should form the opening page and any visitor should be told only to proceed into the site proper if they accept the terms and conditions as stated. For sites of high risk this would be valid advice, but for others it could deter too many visitors to make it, or even the site itself, a viable option. In such cases the disclaimer could form the first few lines of any text or, alternatively, it could be on a separate page connected to the main page by a link with a title like 'Legal Notices'.

However, if this option is taken remember that a link at the bottom of a page is not always visible which could, in this case, leave the company vulnerable. Unless a visitor could be reasonably expected to see the disclaimer it will be considered invalid.

Also remember that it is not always obvious when one website is being left and other being entered. Sometimes the link goes from one page full of information to another which might make for easier web surfing, but which leaves the company at risk. If visitors believe they are still within one website when, in fact, they have moved on then they are viewing content over which the company has absolutely no control, but which would still be attributed to it.

For that reason make it clear when visitors are leaving the company website - and add a disclaimer to the effect that any links are included purely as a convenience and that no responsibility is accepted for their content. Links can be a big enough problem without adding to it.

Links

Here there are two issues: connecting to other sites and the possibility of defamation. To take them in that order. As already stated it is possible to jump from one website to another without being aware of it which has already resulted in legal action more than once.

◆ In October 1996 a newspaper, the 'Shetland News', began extracting headlines from the website of its rival publication, the 'Shetland Times', and inserting them in its own website. As clicking on these headlines took the visitor to the relevant article in the 'Shetland Times' website without informing the visitor of the source of these articles the 'Shetland Times' not unnaturally objected and took out a court injunction preventing the 'Shetland News' from continuing the practice.

◆ In May 1997, according to the magazine PC Pro, the US company Ticketmaster brought an action against Seattle Sidewalk, a web based guide to Seattle owned by Microsoft, claiming that it took visitors into the Ticketmasters website at an inappropriate point.

In both cases it was not so much the link that caused the problem, but the fact that it by-passed the host website's opening page and therefore took visitors away from the advertising placed there.

All of a sudden the issue becomes understandable.

With advertising revenue at stake any company would be prepared to prosecute and so, for that very reason, one simple precaution should be taken. Let the people who own the websites decide which web page any visitors should be directed to. (And check the company website for links coming into the site which similarly by-pass the advertising.)

As to defamation the situation under English law is a lot less clear and all because of a ruling that was made as far back as 1894.

In that year during a local gala a sign was erected libelling a certain Mr Hird who was in dispute with two tradesmen. Furthermore a Mr Wood, for reasons unexplained, spent the day sitting next to the sign directing visitors' attention to it. When Mr Hird sued the court ruled that, as he had directed people to the site, Mr Wood was guilty of publishing it and had therefore libelled Mr Hird.

While that may be a world away from the Internet according to legal experts the principle remains the same. If a company advertises a link to a site which contains defamatory material they could be found equally guilty of defamation. In other words be careful of the sites being linked to, make sure the other site owners accept full responsibility for their content - and talk to a solicitor about legal disclaimers.

There is also one final point which should be mentioned. Any information collected over the Internet is subject to the Data Protection Act which means failing to protect it could result in criminal prosecution. For that reason any company about to go on-line, or already on-line, should include a full review of site security as part of the process.

Summary of points worth considering:

♦ Decide what the website will be used for

♦ Choose an agency, check reference websites

♦ Confirm that any prices quoted will cover design, maintenance and hosting

♦ Make sure the company owns the copyright to the entire website

♦ Decide the content before the site is designed

♦ Agree the site architecture before the site is produced

♦ Remember cultural and language differences

◆   Test the website over the Internet and with more than one Browser

◆   Decide on a link strategy including advertising on other websites

◆   Include a legal disclaimer on the website

Chapter Four

Security Issues

Security is a management problem, but for most people Internet security is perceived as just stopping teenagers from breaking into computers at the Pentagon and accidentally triggering World War Three. This is unfortunate because Internet security is a much more down to earth affair - and should be the concern of every manager. The more so as the Internet is often seen as the natural home for malcontents who, by definition, are highly computer literate. Their activities may, or may not make the headlines, or be the stuff of Hollywood movies, but they can still seriously damage any company which fails to take the right precautions. Fortunately these precautions can be as easily explained as can the threats they are there to guard against.

Active Content

This is the system whereby tiny programs, sometimes known as executable content, create the animations that can now be found on a wide variety of web pages. This is achieved by transferring these programs from the web page to any computer connected to it which then runs the programs just like any other piece of software installed on that computer.

In some cases this is achieved by using the JAVA programming language which calls for another piece of software known as a Virtual Machine or sandbox to be installed on the computer. This then interprets the commands issued by the animation program and passes them through to the computer itself so they can produce whatever special effect the designer created. An alternative to this is Microsoft ActiveX which produces exactly the same effect, but without using a Virtual Machine. Instead the commands issued by these programs, or applets as they are known, are passed straight through to the computer again to do whatever the designer wanted them to do.

As fascinating as these animations might be to watch the security implications are staggering. A program, from an unknown source, can be installed on a computer where it can then issue commands to delete files, alter files or even wipe every file off the hard drive - and all without the knowledge or permission of the user. To make matters worse these applets are not considered to be a computer virus so anti-virus software will neither detect them nor prevent them from operating, yet a maliciously written applet can do every bit as much damage as a maliciously written virus.

Here, in a nutshell, is the problem because some of these JAVA or ActiveX applets are written maliciously. Their sole purpose is to attack any computer which connects itself to their web page. In fact so many attacks of this nature have been reported that it is now possible to categorise these attacks and, in so doing, show exactly what kind of threat any user now faces. These are:

System Modification   Important files are altered.

Invasion of Privacy   Private files can be read.

Denial of Service   Preventing a computer being used for legitimate purposes.

Antagonism   For example continually playing an irritating piece of music until the computer is re-started.

In fairness to Microsoft and Sun (who produce JAVA) they both claim their systems are secure. Microsoft because their ActiveX technology requires each website to have a security certificate without which no computer will accept its applet or program. As far as it goes this is true - except these security certificates can be forged or by-passed easily by the very people who have enough knowledge to write the malicious applets. In much the same way Sun claims that the Virtual Machine which is a requirement for JAVA to work can also screen out any suspicious commands and so protect the computer in that way. This also is true, but only up to a point. In reality loopholes are constantly being found which allow these malicious applets to directly control the computer.

Against a background like that there is only one solution: disable active content. In any Browser this will be one of the options offered and in a corporate environment this should always be taken. Active content in no way adds to the information found on a site, just its appearance, so nothing will be lost by refusing to accept JAVA or ActiveX applets, but a tremendous amount could be saved.

email

Here the strength of the Internet, that any computer can read a message sent by any other, is also its greatest weakness. Any communication sent out over the Internet by email could potentially be read by every single individual with an Internet connection, whether it was addressed to them or not. All it takes is the right software, which can be downloaded from many websites, and company information can be read by anyone who wants to do it. The only counter to this where confidential information is involved is to use some form of file encryption software. Their use can at times be controversial (for which see the Appendix E on governments and the law), but here there is no alternative. Information must be protected and encryption is the only method available.

File Downloads

There are any number of files, better known as programs, which can be downloaded from the Internet and every single one of them carries a security risk. Here the threat comes in two parts: what those files do and what they contain.

Hackers Tools

To take them in that order there are websites on the Internet where so-called hackers tools can be downloaded. This is software specially designed to penetrate security systems which in the wrong hands can be lethal. The rationale behind making these tools freely available is so that systems administrators can use them to check their own systems for any weaknesses which is a fair point (and systems administrators might want to try them out), but no-one else should be allowed to use them on threat of dismissal. With software such as this any number of system settings could be altered which could potentially put the computer out of action until the changes have been rectified - and the cost could be astronomical.

For this reason alone the untrained or the curious must be kept away from these tools. Additionally, of course, there is the added problem of staff being able to access confidential material which is another very good reason for not allowing the software which could make this possible.

Viruses

After that comes the thought that even if these files are perfectly legitimate they might still contain a computer virus. Fortunately this problem can be solved relatively easily as all anti-virus software now comes with an option to check file downloads automatically which, needless to say, should be used. Even so this will not make all files safe as there is something else to be aware of known as a Trojan Horse. Like the horse of legend this is one thing concealed within another. In this case the outer shell of the horse is a program which does whatever it was advertised to do, for example a game or a currency converter, while the Trojan element does something else entirely. Examples here would be altering files, deleting files or even sending company passwords back out over the Internet to be used by whoever created the Trojan Horse in the first place.

Faced with a situation like this the only defence is a ban on all software downloads with the exception of software upgrades from existing suppliers. The key word here being existing; only those software houses where the company already has established trading links should be granted this privilege - and even then the files should be checked for viruses. No other file from no other supplier should be downloaded straight into the company system.

So far the risks under discussion have all been relevant to any company which just wants to surf the Internet (also known as obtaining information from on-line sources). For any company wanting to do no more the threats stop here, but as most companies will probably be thinking in terms of a website at the very least then there are other issues to be considered. Starting with web pages.

Web Pages

Many organisations have found their website hacked into and their web pages altered. In Britain this has happened to all the major political parties while in America it has happened to both the Department of Justice and the CIA. Although in neither case was important information stolen the fact that it could happen at all is a sobering thought, especially as these were far from isolated incidents. Changing web pages is to some as much of a sport as football is to others. Needless to say the more high profile an organisation is, and therefore the more publicity that will be generated by a hacking attack, the more likely it is to be targeted, but that does not mean other sites will be ignored. There are also commercial reasons why a web page would be altered, like discrediting a competitor or stealing customers, so there is no room for complacency.

That said there are a great many ways a website can be altered, in some cases very subtly, so each company should inspect their own website on a regular basis. Points to watch out for are:

- Changes to any pictures or new pictures being substituted.

- Changes to text or new text being substituted.

- Extra comments being added.

- Changes in the links to other web pages taking visitors either to objectionable material or the website of a competitor.

- Changes in contact information such as Name, address, telephone numbers or email address.

- Changes to price or delivery terms for goods and services being offered.

- Changes to the spelling or punctuation which would give the site an unprofessional appearance and so reflect badly on the organisation hosting it.

Whenever a Browser is used it starts by connecting to a named website. Usually this is the website of the company who produced the Browser, but that can be easily changed probably by looking under the section marked preferences. That being the case make the Browser connect to the company website and the above checks can be made each and every time somebody connects to the Internet. It really is that simple.

Unfortunately none of these precautions, or checks, will help the company with a permanent Internet connection; unfortunate because these are the companies at most risk. Due entirely to that Internet connection any hacker in the world is potentially able to steal confidential information off the company computers, and over time many will try unless measures are taken to prevent them. Here there can be no room for complacency.

Any company with a permanent Internet connection must take suitable precautions against hackers, if only to comply with the Data Protection Act which makes failure to adequately protect data a criminal offence.

Robots

To begin with consider the problem of those web robots mentioned in the previous chapter. As they inspect every single site how can they know what information should be made available to the public and what information is confidential? The answer is, because they are told. Any site with information to protect should include a file called ROBOTS.TXT which tells these web robots which areas of the company system to keep away from. Although this file is straightforward to create it should, nevertheless, be done by the design team as here there is no room for mistakes (which is why it should be checked and double checked before the site appears on the Internet).

Also remember that the ROBOTS.TXT file is the Internet equivalent of putting a sign on a door saying 'valuables are inside'. Honest users will stay away, but for the dishonest it just tells them where to look so extra security must be included in the original website budget.

Here the most common form of protection is by the use of a device known as a firewall.

Firewalls

A firewall is defined as a system, or group of systems, which enforces access control between two networks. In plain English something that monitors all communication between the company network and the Internet and makes sure that this communication is legitimate. Broadly speaking there are two main types of firewall: network level and application level.

Network Level Firewalls

These accept or reject messages based on the source address of that message. To explain, every message is split up into smaller packets of data before being sent out over the Internet. Naturally this packet of data carries its destination address so any computer it passes through knows where to send it next, however it also carries the source address which is what the network level firewall looks for. If the data packet originates from a known, or pre-defined, address it is let through into the company system; if not it is rejected.

Network level firewalls are what is known as transparent to the user which means no-one knows they are there. They operate without the users being aware of their existence. While this can make them popular they are by no means the best solution for high security organisations as they can be defeated. It is possible to forge the source address on data packets and so fool the firewall into thinking they come from an approved source. A practice known in the trade as IP Spoofing (From TCP/IP, which is explained in Appendix B).

Application Level Firewalls

These perform a much more sophisticated analysis of the data passing through them according to criteria set by each individual company. Although more secure this auditing process takes time which means the system will run that much slower.

Additionally it could require extra training on the part of the user.

As a further refinement both types of firewall could be used in combination. Low grade information could be protected by a network level firewall to take advantage of its speed while high grade information could be protected behind an application level firewall to take advantage of its greater security. In this way a great deal of safety can be built into the system - and yet security will still not be absolute. Firewalls cannot prevent a virus being downloaded nor are they proof against sabotage or stupidity from personnel within the company.

Something else a firewall cannot do is set the security policy for the company. They are without doubt the physical representation of that security policy, and they work according to the guidelines laid down in that same security policy, but they cannot create it themselves. Only humans can do that.

Security Policy

The best method of defence when dealing with the Internet could be described as enlightened paranoia: assume everything is a threat unless, or until, it can be proved otherwise. This means start by restricting all access and all Internet services unless a case can be made for their use on an individual basis. Just because one service is allowed does not mean similar services should be automatically allowed at the same time. After that draw up guidelines which will answer the following questions:

- Should all incoming email be allowed, or just that coming from known sites?

- Should outgoing email be allowed to any destination, or should it be restricted to specific addresses?

- Should data be transferred anywhere, or just to specific sites?

- Should data be received from anywhere, or just from specific sites?

- Should total access to the World Wide Web be allowed, or should it be restricted to specific sites?

By answering these questions a workable security policy can be drawn up. This should then be written in clear, unambiguous, terms and a copy given to every member of staff. Because of the importance of data security it is usually recommended that every staff member should sign a document stating that they have received this policy document and that they understand that any transgressions could lead to disciplinary measures or even dismissal. In companies who might have to enforce this ruling it would be better if a lawyer was consulted over the exact wording to prevent the company being later sued for unfair dismissal.

Should that seem a very heavy handed approach a gentler alternative is to invest in a specialist software package which restricts access to the more objectionable, or dangerous, websites. There are a great many of these on the market so the choice is wide, but do not rely on them unconditionally. Like the firewall they have to be configured to match individual circumstances and, also like firewalls, their effectiveness needs to be carefully monitored. Equally, they cannot be set up properly until the above questions have been answered and a valid security policy established.

Finally, always remember that a security policy is not an end in itself. It is merely the means to an end which, in this case, means a safe and secure computer system. In other words do not just write the security policy and then file it away as a job done. If company information and the computers that hold it are to be protected there is only one way to treat a security policy: live by it.

Summary of points worth considering:

♦ Disable active content (JAVA and ActiveX)

♦ Confidential emails should be encrypted

♦ Ban all file downloads except for software updates

♦ Regularly check the company website for hacking attacks

♦ If company computers are permanently connected to the Internet install a firewall

♦ Set a security policy - and live by it

Chapter Five

Electronic Trading

To many people trading on the Internet with your website is the cutting edge of the Internet, certainly it seems to be where the hype is concentrated at the moment. As ever, of course, most of the stories are only partially true at most and yet on information such as this managers are expected to allocate significant financial resources. Not only that but these same managers could then stand accused when their particular company venture fails to make the vast fortunes being earned by other websites, according to press reports at least.

Just so the point is well made remember the GartnerGroup report on website ventures which was quoted earlier. 75% fail to produce the returns expected. Internet commerce is not the proverbial licence to print money despite what the hype merchants say. Instead, like any other venture, it requires careful thought and a well researched business plan. Without that any company would do better to give the money to charity rather than spend it on a website. At least then some good would come of it.

That said, now is the time to look at how money can be made on the Internet. What follows then is only a very simple guide to starting what the media are increasingly referring to as an e-business. While it is unlikely to provide all the answers if nothing else it should raise the right questions which can then be asked of others.

Of these the first is connectivity.

Connectivity

The first requirement for any website is that it must be available twenty-four hours a day seven days a week (or 24x7 as it is known). The next is that any company which owns a website must have immediate access to it or else how can the orders be processed. These two are related in that it all comes down to how is the company connected to the Internet and where is its website hosted.

Leased Line

The easiest although the most expensive option is to have a leased line from the company network to the Internet via the ISP. If this is done most problems disappear, but the cost of this means that the website will need a healthy turnover just to break even. Given that a significant part of the cost will be the leased line some money can be saved by using an ISP in the same geographical area which could be worth investigating. (A leased line to the other side of town will always be cheaper than a leased line to the other side of the country.) On the plus side, of course, being stored on the company's own computer the website will always be available for maintenance and orders taken by it can be easily transferred into the company system.

Use a Web Hosting Service

Next in price is to make use of a company which specialises in web hosting; they rent out space on their computers which are permanently connected to the Internet. While this is cheaper than using a company computer there are still security considerations to bear in mind which means the hosting company should be made to answer the same questions an ISP was asked regarding both security and reliability.

Board and Lodge

Assuming a cheaper option is required a viable alternative could be what is sometimes referred to as board and lodge. A computer owned by the company is stored on the premises of the ISP. This computer can then be permanently connected to the Internet and also accessed by the company through a simple dial up connection. While cheaper than a leased line the ISP would still charge for storing that computer on its premises so it is hardly cost free, especially as other conditions would very likely be imposed.

Rent ISP Space

A fourth, and even cheaper option, is to rent space on the ISP's own computer. (Its web server.) This can be done easily and could perhaps best be described as the toe in the water option. If the website proves unsuccessful the losses will have been kept to a minimum while if it is a success the other options can be considered. In fact on that point if it is a success the company will most likely have no other choice but to consider its options. The ISP would insist on it to prevent one client from using too much of the available resources at the expense of others.

Of these perhaps the most important concerns the question of maintenance and repair, either to the computer itself or to the software installed on it which would be entirely the responsibility of the company not the ISP. On the face of it this might not seem like much of a problem, except the ISP would very likely insist on an appointment being made before allowing company representatives to visit their own computer. As no-one would be happy with a situation where total strangers could arrive unannounced at the premises of an ISP and be given immediate access to the computers stored there this is obviously a necessary security measure, just so long as the consequences can be lived with. And in this case the consequences are that if the computer, or its software, developed a fault it could be several days before repair work could begin; days when that website could potentially be out of commission.

Integration

Any business wanting to sell off a web page must also consider how this will integrate with its existing system. In other words as that website is another sales outlet how will those sales be handled. Also remember that before placing an order these potential E-Customers (for want of a better term) might also need to know if a part is in stock or, if not, when can a delivery be made and it soon becomes apparent that at the very least some basic stock control system must be linked to the web page. And this is on top of linking the web page to the order entry system. In all cases, of course, managers face a dilemma which can never be resolved because the information to do that will only be there after any decisions are taken.

On the one hand if nothing is done, if no attempt at integration is made, then any orders taken by the website will have to be printed out and physically entered into the sales ordering system. Where a large number of sales are concerned this could overload the entire sales department to the point where huge backlogs of unprocessed orders could build up, causing a great deal of customer dissatisfaction. Alternatively if a lot of effort and money is spent integrating the company systems it would all be wasted if those sales failed to materialise.

In October 1999 GartnerGroup carried out a survey which found that for every £1 spent on a website anywhere between £5 and £50 needed to be spent on integration so this is obviously something that needs careful thought. The wide variation in cost coming from the wide variation in the complexity of the systems needing integration.

To make matters worse this is also an area where the experts disagree. There are those who say no E-Commerce should be attempted without full systems integration while others are just as certain that the E-Commerce should begin immediately with integration taking place later, should it be needed. Cynically, this means that any decisions taken will always have expert backing, but it is hardly an ideal situation considering the risks involved. Fortunately a small amount of common sense can point the way to other options although it has to be said neither of them is perfect.

Small Scale Start-up

Instead of selling an entire range of products off the website start by offering just one or two. This will need no integration of systems as the sales should be low enough to be handled manually. Later, of course, once the website has been in operation long enough for an accurate assessment to be made then any decisions can be taken based on solid information instead of guesswork and optimism.

Incremental Integration

Instead of connecting every system to the website connect just the barest minimum to make it work efficiently. For example the sales ordering system could be connected (integrated) to the website while everything else from Stock Control to Invoicing could be handled manually. Equally, depending on the goods being sold, it might be that stock information is needed on the website while order processing can be left until later. Anything is possible as a short term measure until the information is available to make long term decisions.

No matter what the route taken towards integration there is still a lot more to the subject than that - and all of it is important.

To begin with remember that any existing computer systems might not integrate easily with the website operation. Brand new software might be needed in addition to what is already being used or even to replace it completely. Either way this will have to be done long before that website goes live if only to deal with any teething troubles that are always present whenever new systems are introduced. If not just imagine trying to deal with a brand new computer system and an E-Commerce system all at the same time. Better yet imagine having to deal with all the unhappy customers, unhappy unions and unhappy staff which would be the end result.

Next, but by no means less important, is the fact that when all the company systems are fully integrated there will be what might be described as an electronic pathway running from the Internet to all the confidential or commercially sensitive information stored on the company's computers. The path might not be straightforward, and it might not even be there intentionally, but it will be there. It has to be. Once all the systems are interconnected access to one automatically gives access to them all and hackers anywhere in the world could exploit that fact.

In short, whenever even partial integration of systems is being talked about security must be at the top of the agenda. Long before that website becomes operational every reasonable precaution must be in place to guard against the theft or alteration of company data. Anything less than that could in a very real sense put the entire company in danger. Furthermore, as failure to adequately protect personal data is an offence against the Data Protection Act it could even put the directors of that company in jail. With security as with any other aspect of going on-line planning is an absolute necessity - especially when systems are being integrated.

Hardware

When a company system, or a company network, is connected to the Internet via a website the amount of data passing through that system can increase dramatically. While that may be expected, even hoped for, it can still put the entire system under an incredible strain. It therefore makes sense to check that the hardware side of the system can cope. If not that too must be upgraded and the cost included in the website business plan. Here it is best to take an optimistic view of how many customers will visit the website and plan accordingly. Having spare capacity will never be a problem for any network, but not having enough could stifle the web business right from the very beginning.

Function

Even under the general topic of trade a website can still have a variety of different functions. Some can be a simple on-line catalogue allowing cust-omers to buy products off the shelf while others can offer a more bespoke service; guiding potential customers through the product range to find the right choice for their particular requirements. As this affects the complexity of the website which, in turn, affects the design costs the actual function of the site should be decided long in advance. Considering how high the start up costs can sometimes be there should be no place for snap decisions.

Location

A website need not necessarily stand alone waiting for visitors to find it. It could just as easily be part of a so-called cyber mall. These are in effect a collection of different websites all linked together through one single web page. Typically this page would show a graphical representation of a high street where clicking on each individual shop front would lead directly to that particular website. As these cyber malls will also have their own advertising to attract customers to them this could be a good way of increasing business.

Those ISPs who are also content providers usually have their own cyber malls which could be worth investigating. While the customer base is likely to be restricted to the clients of that ISP, so they can provide a wider range of content to their subscribers as a way of attracting more, this can have its compensations. The ISP will want to advertise this new service which is another way of saying it will advertise the website in ways many companies would never be able to afford.

Payment

For any company this is the major concern: how will they be paid? It could well be that the nature of the goods being sold means that this is not an issue. Many websites take orders over the Internet and then expect the customer to pay on receipt like a home delivery pizza (which can be ordered off a website). Alternatively, of course, the customer could just be invoiced in the normal way. In either case payment is not a problem, but it becomes a very big problem when money has to be taken off an anonymous web surfer living in some other part of the world. One solution is electronic cash or ecash.

Ecash

Here money is transferred from a normal bank account into an electronic cash account which can then be used to buy goods on-line. With ecash no-one has to send their credit card details over the Internet, but the drawback is that the money must be in the account before they can spend it which means paying in advance. A further drawback is that anyone who opens an account with one ecash company is restricted to buying only off the websites which accept that particular brand of ecash. If their ecash is supplied by a different company they will be unable to buy off that website. For this reason anyone who is planning to accept ecash on their website would be well advised to find out how many other clients the ecash company has before signing up for the service. The more it has the more likely it is that people will want to use its ecash. At the same time they should also ask how long it will take before they are paid for any goods bought as in some cases this settlement period can be in excess of ninety days.

Despite its drawbacks ecash can be the perfect medium for sites selling small value items where a credit card would be inappropriate. As such the economics could be worth investigating.

As for higher priced purchases the only solution available is credit cards and that brings with it a whole range of security issues (covered later in this chapter). Everything from protecting the card number while it is in transit over the Internet to protecting the seller against the fraudulent use of a stolen credit card have to be considered, alongside several other points in between. It was to address some of these problems that Netscape introduced a scheme known as Secure Sockets Layer or SSL.

Secure Sockets Layer (SSL)

Under this system the credit card number is encrypted before it is sent out over the Internet to keep it safe. Only the intended recipient can decode it, a piece of magic that is performed by using what are known as digital certificates.

First any company wanting to use this SSL technology must apply for a certificate from what is known as a Certificate Authority or CA. This certificate, which is actually a piece of software, is then installed on the company website to create a secure area. Depending entirely on where the website is hosted this might involve extra costs as some ISPs could charge an administration fee if the website is on their computer. However, with or without that the site is now open for business.

When potential customers then visit this site their Browser will automatically know it is secure, mainly because that information will be sent to them alongside everything else that makes up a web page. This will also be displayed to the user in the form of a small icon on the Browser itself. Netscape Navigator shows a stylised picture of a key, if the key is broken the site is insecure while a whole key means a secure site. In Microsoft Internet Explorer the picture is of an open or closed padlock. Should a visitor then want to buy off that site their digital certificate, which they must also apply for, encrypts their credit card details before sending such information out over the Internet.

There is slightly more to it than that as the buyer's digital certificate also sends extra information to confirm the identity of the buyer concerned. This can then be checked at the receiving end i.e. by the seller. If the identity as stated on the digital certificate does not match that as stated on the credit card then the card is most likely being used fraudulently and the transaction can be prevented. Although this seems to give protection only to the seller the buyer too is safeguarded. Firstly because the digital certificates are only given to legitimately registered companies and secondly because they can be removed from any company should a doubt exist as to its trading standards.

On the face of it, then, SSL would appear to be the answer the whole of the Internet commerce industry has been looking for - except it has one glaring weakness. The merchant server, otherwise known as the computer hosting the selling company's website, must store both these credit card numbers and the identity of the people who own them. Should security there ever be compromised the consequences could be catastrophic. In which case why would anyone want to take the risk with their credit card? It was to answer such worries that led to the creation of a different system known as Secure Electronic Transaction or SET.

Secure Electronic Transaction (SET)

This also uses digital certificates, which also come from Certificate Authorities, but here another organisation known as a proxy merchant is also involved. The idea is that buyers send their, suitably encrypted, credit card details to the proxy merchant which performs the same identity check as for SSL. Assuming everything is in order this proxy merchant then sends an authorisation to the seller, but withholds the credit card details. From the point of view of the seller they have the go-ahead to complete the transaction, they will get paid, while the actual details of the credit card are, to them, irrelevant. All they need to know is that the card is genuine. It is therefore only the proxy merchant which can match credit card details to name and addresses.

This might seem like transferring the problem rather than solving it as there will still exist a computer file holding extremely valuable credit card details, but the safety here lies in the quantity of those files. Instead of potentially millions of websites each holding credit card details there will be just a small number where the security can be guaranteed; something that cannot always be said of other websites. By concentrating the information together in this way it can be guarded by organisations where security is of paramount concern and taken care of by experts. In fact the latest boast from the companies involved with SET is that their information is protected by encryption routines stronger than those used by the military to protect nuclear launch codes. (So if SET security is ever broken the world might have more to worry about than a banking scandal.)

Given that SET is being backed by MasterCard, Visa and American Express not to mention Microsoft and Netscape the chances are high that this will be adopted throughout the Internet. As such any company who wants to trade off their website has very little choice but to take an interest.

Finally, for anyone wondering where on the computer will all these digital certificates be stored the answer is simple: in an ewallet. These are now included as standard in the latest versions of all the Browsers.

Now that what might best be described as the theory has been dealt with it becomes time to consider more practical matters. Exactly how can anyone set up their own e-commerce website. The first, and easiest, way of setting up an e-commerce website is to throw money at it. Outside consultants can be brought in or companies specialising in e-commerce solutions can be approached. Then just sit back and let it happen. By far the easiest it might be, but it is also the most expensive. In which case what follows is for people who lack such deep pockets. People, in other words, who have to do it themselves. Here the first point to consider is payment. How will a company be paid for goods bought off a website?

Credit Card Payment

In practice this means the ability to accept credit cards. In even more practical terms any company that wants to sell goods off its website must be granted merchant status by a credit card company. Many companies may already have this set up, but they need to inform their bank that they now also want an Internet credit card facility. Fortunately this is nowhere near as complicated as it sounds. Just get in touch with a credit card company, fill in the forms and pay a small admin fee. There is nothing else to it although several points do need to be kept in mind.

Of these, the first is that - despite rumours - companies do not need two or three years of audited accounts before merchant status will be granted. The credit card companies have now all embraced the dot com world at least to the point where they are prepared to grant merchant status even to start-ups. Of course, that is subject to other conditions being met which is where the problems start.

To begin with, and for obvious reasons, the credit card company must be satisfied those credit card details will be stored with a sufficient degree of security. At the very least this will call for the files holding those credit card details to be encrypted. There will also be a lot of probing questions about company security in general so be prepared to answer these. For anyone who wants to be granted merchant status, lax security is not an option.

Next comes more general terms of trading which is where even well managed companies can fall down badly. The problem here is if the website is more successful than anticipated, leading to a backlog of orders building up. Under these circumstances a customer could see items charged to their credit card statement weeks, even months, before they see the goods. Needless to say they will then complain to the credit card company who, just as naturally, will take the matter up with the owners of the website. And the conversation will be far from sympathetic. In extreme cases merchant status could even be withdrawn. While that would be the final nail in the coffin of any website venture in truth the project would be dead long before then. Once the word spread both the company and the website would acquire such a bad reputation that no-one would want to do business with it. (And on the Internet the word spreads at the speed of electricity through wire.)

The point of all this is that every company should have a contingency plan to cover unexpectedly high demand. Not only will the credit card companies insist on one before granting merchant status, but by not planning for this eventuality a company could lose far more than just a few credit card sales. It also must be said that any e-commerce system should be set up so that credit cards are billed only on despatch of goods. That way even if there is a delay at least the credit card company will have nothing to complain about. The customer will, of course, which is why a contingency plan is such a good idea.

In short a lot of work has to be done before merchant status is granted. In many cases, with small companies, it may well be that the work and expense involved cannot be justified by the expected returns from the website. Under those circumstances a proxy merchant should be used.

Proxy Merchants

These have already been mentioned in the section covering SET. Even so there is more to the business of using proxy merchants. This is another area where, unless the sums are done properly, money can be lost rather than made. The first consideration is, how much commission will be charged on each sale. Although this is negotiable as it also includes the commission being charged by the credit card company a small company could find itself paying anything up to 9% of the total value of each sale. Fairly obviously that could have a serious impact on the profitability of any web project which is why the sums need doing. Know in advance how much commission the company can afford. Then negotiate.

Another point to be considered is the payment terms, which are not negotiable. Here, as the proxy merchant will always wait until the credit card company pays them, there could be a 60 day gap between the despatch of goods and those goods being paid for. Exactly how much of an impact that has on company cash flow will obviously depend on individual circumstances, but it should definitely be included in the business plan.   Finally, for anyone wondering how to locate a proxy merchant the answer is simple: search the Internet.

Software

Before anything can be sold off a website, that website must first be created. Here, there are a number of options available. However, on the assumption that turning everything over to a web design agency is too expensive now is the time to consider an off-the-shelf package.

In fact there are now several software packages designed to do no more than create e-commerce websites - and all of them aimed at the amateur. Using these involves virtually no more than entering the price and description of whatever goods are being offered and then letting the software build a website. These websites may not be as sophisticated as some, but they do the job which is what really counts. Remember, when it comes to e-commerce the golden rule is that the website is there to create sales, not to impress geeks with all manner of special effects.

For anyone who wants to see any of these packages in action the best idea is to surf the net. Look at a few e-commerce sites, not with a view to buying but just to see what kind of features the site has to offer and how easy it is to navigate. Then send a polite email to the site owners asking what package they used to create it. Quite apart from the time saved in evaluating various software packages there is every chance the communication could lead to a mutually beneficial exchange of links. And yet there is still more to Internet trading than simply selling goods off a website. There is also such a thing as Electronic Data Interchange otherwise known as EDI.

Electronic Data Interchange (EDI)

Although not strictly an Internet technology EDI is included here as it involves companies trading with each other electronically which could involve the use of the Internet. Furthermore as EDI is essentially a way of linking the purchasing system of one company with the inventory and manufacturing system of another, which is increasingly coming into the province of what the media is describing as eCommerce, no discussion of electronic trading would be complete without at least mentioning it.

EDI is defined as 'the exchange of information in a standard format between one organisation's computer application and another using electronic means'. While most of this is self-explanatory the phrase 'standard format' does deserve more of an explanation. This is because EDI does not use the standard TCP/IP of the Internet, but instead uses its own system.

To be more exact it uses several systems for different industries although that is now starting to change with the introduction of an international standard known as EDIFACT or EDI for Administration, Commerce and Transport.

In plain English EDI is simply a system whereby one company raises a purchase order which is sent to the relevant supplier electronically. The supplier in question then accepts this order into its sales system and from there it is passed either to a warehouse for despatch or to manufacturing so the items can be produced.

And all of this happens electronically, no paperwork is raised. Futuristic it might be, but there are many companies who are seeing a competitive advantage in using it such as lower inventory costs, lower administration costs and therefore improved cash flow. However, as these benefits can only be realised when both customer and supplier integrate their systems, this is not something that any company can undertake alone. For that reason to go any further would be beyond the scope of this book.

Summary of points worth considering:

◆ The website must be continually available so orders can be processed

◆ The website can be located in-house, with a web hosting company or with the ISP

◆ The website must be integrated with the company system

◆   Integration issues can be partially solved either by a small scale start up or by having only partial integration

◆   Confirm the company computers can handle the extra load

◆   A website could be part of a cybermall

◆   Decide how payment for goods sold will be made

Chapter Six

Marketing A Website

No matter how good a website might be the entire effort will be wasted if no-one knows it exists. For this reason the marketing of a website is as important as its design. All of which explains this chapter. In some cases it may go over ground already covered, but take that as a measure of how important this subject really is. A website without visitors is not worth having.

Paid for Advertising

The first, and obvious, way to let everyone know a website exists is to tell them by means of paid-for advertising. Expensive it might be, but it does work. To be more exact it can work, providing a few points are kept in mind. Of these the first few assumes the advertising will be done using a medium other than the Internet. After that Internet advertising needs to be considered, but first, media advertising.

Media Advertising

Radio

As is probably known already this is limited only by the size of the budget. Television, radio, newspapers and magazines are all be prepared to carry adverts for websites. The only slight problem here is with radio and that only because the people listening will most likely not be prepared to write down a web address mentioned in an advert. Because of this radio advertising should only be used if the web address is both instantly memorable and easy to spell. To see why that might be imagine a website which had the address GUDBIZ.COM. Memorable it may be, but how many people would know how to spell it if they only ever heard the name spoken on the radio? Even if that same address was repeated in newspaper or magazine adverts, where the correct spelling could be seen, paying for one advert which depended on people seeing another advert in print will never be an effective way of spending the advertising budget.

Traditional Areas

There is also another aspect of media advertising which needs to be considered. This is where a company has more than just a website to be promoted, where it has products to be sold through more traditional outlets. Under these circumstances a website should be used as part of an overall marketing strategy. In this way an advert could include a comment such as; 'For more information visit our website'. Not only does this advertise both the product and the website, it also means the advert can concentrate purely on selling the product. Information about the product can be placed on the company website. Given that storing information on a website will always be far, far, cheaper than placing that same information inside a media advert the benefits should be obvious, especially if the product could be bought off that same website. (Even so be careful, not everyone has Internet access and yet they might still need further information before buying the product. Use the website as a supplementary source of information, not the only source.)

This does, of course, presuppose that the website is capable of being constantly adapted to suit the latest marketing campaign which can only happen if it was designed that way right from the beginning. Yet further proof that the person in charge of a web based project must be fully aware of both corporate strategy and corporate objectives.

Internet Advertising

Without stretching the point too much it could be said that establishing a link with another website is a form of advertising. After all, once the links are established there will be other places on the Internet where the company website is mentioned. A good link strategy can, therefore, pay dividends.

Be creative. Think of the people your website is aimed at. What are their interests, what are their aspirations, what other websites are they likely to visit and what are they most likely to look for on the Internet? The answer to all of those questions will help to find the right websites where a link could draw paying customers to your site.

Of course, some of these sites will only be interested in, paid-for, banner advertising rather than a free link which is to be expected. Websites do have to be paid for. On the plus side, however, advertising a website on another website is a sure way of reaching only those people who have Internet access; something that cannot be guaranteed when advertising in other media. Internet advertising also has one other major benefit. The results of that advertising can be monitored to an extent previously unheard of. Better yet that monitoring can be used to produce an increasingly effective advertising strategy.

When a visitor arrives at a particular website it is a simple matter to determine the site they visited immediately prior to that. (The ISP or web hosting company can help.) Then all it takes is to match this information against a list of websites holding links or banner advertising and it will be immediately obvious which is the most effective, and least effective, method of bringing visitors to the website. E-commerce websites can even take that a stage further and include what those visitors bought and how much money they spent.

Armed with information like that it becomes a simple matter to refine any advertising strategy; discarding ineffective sites and actively seeking out websites similar to those bringing in the most, or highest spending, customers. Furthermore, if this analysis is carried out on a regular basis then the advertising strategy can become ever more refined and ever more precisely targeted. It may take a few months, but eventually the visitors should start to arrive in satisfactory numbers.

So, while paid-for advertising does involve spending yet more money on top of that already spent to create the website it can produce results. Even so there is another way of getting the company website mentioned by the media and, this time, it costs not a single penny.

Editorial

The best place for any website to be mentioned is in the editorial pages of newspapers and magazines. Not only does this carry more authority than paid-for advertising, it is also free. A set of circumstances which should interest any company.

To generate this golden publicity start by creating a press release.

This should include:

- The name and address of the company

- A contact name if more information is required

- The address of the website

- The purpose of the website

- A brief explanation as to why this website is newsworthy

After that either fax or post this to the editor of any and every relevant publication. (Do not send it email as busy editors like to keep that channel free for urgent communications and are likely to ignore anything else.) In this context, of course, a relevant publication could be the local media, who are usually willing to help local companies.

Alternatively it could be major national newspapers, who all have Internet sections these days, or any magazine which serves the same market the website is intended for. Anything is possible. All it takes is a little bit of creativity to think of a reason why a website should be newsworthy. Everything else can be left to the fact that every publication imaginable will always be hungry for content. They want stories about websites every bit as much as that website wants to be written about.

There are, of course, other ways of getting a website noticed than by relying on the media. Some are obvious, some less so, but all of them should be considered. No commercial website can have too much publicity.

In no particular order of importance these alternative methods are:

Self-Promotion

This is both easy to explain and should be done by every company regardless of size or budget. Quite simply, every document that company produces should have the address of its website heavily featured. From sales brochure to purchase order and from business card to invoice the website must be included. Going on from there that website should be mentioned in every advert, it should be included on any promotional items like pens or coffee mugs and if it is possible to show the web address on whatever product is being sold it should be seen there too.

In short, take every opportunity to tell the world about the company website. Doing it is practically cost free so the results can only be positive.

Extra Websites

This is a clever form of marketing that is possible only on the Internet. It is easy, effective and, best of all, it is cheap. As an example of how it works imagine a company called, say, Smith Ltd which produces Alpha Widgets. While Smith Ltd may have a website under its own name there is absolutely nothing to stop it having a second website called ALPHAWIDGETS.COM. This second website need be no more than a single page holding a brief description of the product and a link taking visitors to the main company website and yet think of the benefits:

♦   When potential customers search the Internet an extra website is an extra chance the company name will be returned

♦   An extra website can be indexed by search engines under its own key words, increasing the chances of being found by potential customers still further

♦   An extra website is an extra link to the main website which will improve its relevancy ranking with any search engine that takes links into account

♦   An extra website could have links of its own to other websites, helping to direct customers to the main company website

To explain that last point imagine a small publisher which sold its books on-line. Also imagine that it published a book called 'The Garden' and had registered the title of that book as a website, THEGARDEN.COM. This website could be no more than the blurb taken straight off the back cover of the book, its price and a link to the company e-commerce site. Yet it would still be a website in its own right. It could, therefore, also have another link to a garden furniture website, for example. If it did, then anybody visiting that garden furniture website could follow a link to the book website and from there they could be taken directly to the publisher's e-commerce website. In this way new customers could be conjured up practically out of thin air.

A company can have as many websites as it wants. In the example above that publishing company could register the title of every book it published as a website - and they could all have links to many other sites. Equally a manufacturer could register the brand name of every single one of its products. Not only is this perfectly legitimate, but the cost of registering a domain name (website) is far cheaper than any other form of advertising.

To use a slightly fanciful analogy. If the customer is a fish then trying to catch that fish with a single website is like using a rod and line. Multiple websites, each with their own links, would be like trawling for fish with a large net. When it comes to commercial web projects it is always better to be a professional fisherman than a riverside angler.

Giveaways

Giving something away for free is a sure way of persuading people to visit a website. Obviously the fact that something was being given away free would have to be advertised so this is hardly a cost free option, especially when the cost of the free gift is added to the equation, but it is still effective. Everyone likes the thought of something for nothing.   The only question remaining is, what can be offered? Here expert opinion varies. Some say it should be a small piece of software like a screensaver or currency converter, except that would only work if visitors were using their own home computers. An office user should be following a policy which forbids downloads of any kind, making the offer pointless. Therefore, before trying this strategy, think of the target audience - and whose computer they will be using to do their web surfing.

Alternatively try offering something other than software, like information. This could be a specially commissioned report, the results of a market survey, technical information or anything else. If a company possesses information which would be of interest to others it could be placed on the website as an inducement to visitors. Giving away information might go against the grain of corporate culture, but it does work.

Competitions

This is another area where expert advice seems to be aimed more at large companies than small. First of all it has to be said that a competition on a website, like some form of on-line quiz, will help to attract visitors. The question is, how much will it all cost. In fact sites exist telling people which sites to visit to win prizes.

A competition has to be designed, it has to be advertised and someone has to go through the responses to choose a winner. Even before the prize is considered all of this can be expensive. True, as competitors will have to leave their email address so the winner can be contacted, this will create a valuable marketing resource, but it is still a strategy for those whose budget is big enough to cope. Smaller companies would be better advised to try different tactics.

Questionnaire

This is more a way of refining an existing advertising or marketing strategy. A way of finding out exactly who is visiting a website. To do it add a questionnaire to a website which can include such things as :

- Age
- Income bracket
- Gender
- Nationality
- How the site was found
- Could they navigate the site easily
- What were they looking for
- Were their needs met
- Ideas from them for improvement

Be careful about such questions as ethnic origin or sexual orientation. These are highly sensitive subjects and some people might not want to answer questions on them. They might not like even being asked.

Also, be aware that under the terms of the 1998 Data Protection Act the website must include an explanation as to why this information is being collected. (To provide a better service to customers is a valid reason, but it must be stated.) It must also state to what uses this information will be put. (Again, marketing and improving service levels are valid reasons.) Finally, any information collected must be for company use only and must never be passed on to any third parties without the express permission of the individuals concerned.

A great deal of useful information can be collected from a website questionnaire. Just be sure the process of collecting it does not lead to a heavy fine or jail sentence.

There are many ways of marketing a website; some expensive, some cheap. They all work and they all should be tried as far as the budget will allow. More than that they should be used continually. Website marketing is not a one-off exercise. With so many websites on the Internet unless yours is promoted constantly it will be lost in the crowd.

Summary of points worth considering:

◆   Advertising is expensive, but effective

◆   Only use radio advertising if the name of the website is memorable and easy to spell

◆   Websites can be used as part of a wider marketing strategy

◆   Links with other websites are a form of advertising

◆   Advertising on the Internet can be carefully monitored

◆   Press releases can help to generate further publicity

◆   Include the website address on all company documents

◆   Register extra websites and develop a link strategy for them

◆   Try giving away something for free on the website

◆   Try holding competitions on the website

◆   Website questionnaires can be useful

◆   Promote the website constantly

Chapter Seven

Intranets, Tele-Working and the Virtual Corporation

This chapter could practically be subtitled 'things to do with the Internet' as that, broadly speaking, is its theme. While it could be argued that was also the theme of the entire book in this particular chapter the focus will not so much be on the hows and whys of using the Internet as on what tech-nology is available to extend its reach into other areas of corporate activity.

For some that may be a very worrying thought. The Internet already seems to be all pervasive, and knowing that the topics covered here are all the latest industry buzzwords is unlikely to allay too many of those fears. Buzzwords are by their very nature the latest thing which means they come shrouded in hype, jargon and the kind of uninformed guesses that can only be made when a product is too new for anyone to collect statistics about its usage. For that reason every warning given about the Internet applies equally here. The technology has yet to prove itself in practice to the extent necessary to justify some of the claims being made for it. Even so those claims are being made and as not all of them are based on wishful thinking it would be as well to know what these new technologies involve. They could be the way of the future.

Intranets

Despite what was said earlier, Intranets are based on mature technology, or as mature as it gets in the IT industry. In fact this is simply the Internet as applied to a company network. To put that another way, imagine all the computers owned by the company being connected to each other in exactly the same way as computers all over the world are connected to each other by the Internet. That would then be a company Intranet. There are other differences, obviously, of which the first is that this company Intranet, or network, does not necessarily have to be connected to the Internet proper. It could perfectly easily exist in total isolation from the rest of the world. There would also have to be extra software added to each computer so that the information stored on it would, in effect, be set up as the equivalent to a website complete with links to other web pages, but this could be easily done. The technology which creates web pages for the Internet can also create web pages for a company Intranet because the system is exactly the same. It even uses the same HTML coding and is designed to be accessed by the same Browsers.

As far as Intranets are concerned the only real questions to be answered are not those of implementation, but the much more practical concerns such as why would anyone want to do it in the first place? Here the original idea was that it could be used in situations where large numbers of people needed access to large amounts of constantly updated information. For example companies selling a wide variety of components (like automobile spares) would be spared the expense of constantly re-printing their parts list every time a price or specification changed. Instead the entire catalogue could be stored on a web page where any updates would be as easy as pressing the right button. There was also talk of large organisations storing their internal phone directories on an Intranet for exactly the same reason although neither of these uses was enough to turn Intranets into something more than just a theoretical possibility. Standard computer networks already offered most of this, but as Browsers and web pages slowly became more sophisticated an unexpected side-effect of this was to make Intranets more useful so that other, major, advantages now exist. These are:

There Is No Need to Know the Location of a Document

On a standard computer network any user has to know where a particular document is stored before they can use it. As this involves knowing not just which particular directory or sub-directory the document is stored in, but also which computer hard drive that directory is on. This can be a time consuming and endlessly frustrating task. Intranet technology solves this as simply clicking on a relevant link takes a user directly to the document concerned the way it works on any other web page on the Internet.

Audit Trails are Created

The system that allows websites to record details of anyone visiting that site can also be applied to Intranets. This means there can be an audit trail leading from an individual user to each and every document they accessed. From a security point of view alone this is invaluable with the added advantage that Systems Administrators can use the same information for the kind of usage analysis they need to keep the network running efficiently (or to prove they need more equipment).

Access Levels Can Be Infinitely Variable

In exactly the same way that a website, or pages on that website, can be restricted to people with the right authorisation so too can documents on a company Intranet. A standard network can restrict access to a particular directory, but anyone who is allowed to use that directory has automatic access to every file on it whether they need that information or not.

With an Intranet this can be prevented. The technology that allows for a particular password or ID to be entered before a web page becomes available can be applied to individual documents on an Intranet to create an infinitely variable access control policy. Users are restricted to just those documents they need and no other.

In-house Training is Facilitated

The interactive nature of web pages makes it an ideal medium for staff training. There are also those who recommend that a company Intranet scheme should be implemented before going on-line with a full blown Internet project. The idea being that as the two technologies are so similar the experience gained with the former will be invaluable when the latter is introduced.

Document Management Systems are Possible

If company documents are transferred to CD-ROM they can be retrieved over the Intranet far easier than if they were stored on paper and kept in filing cabinets. For companies with a large amount of documents there is even a device known as a juke box which, like the original juke box, can store many disks. When a particular disk is needed it is played automatically. Because of this Intranets are seen as bringing the so-called paperless office one step closer.

Hardware Costs Could Be Reduced

As office application software like word processors or spreadsheets could be taken directly from a web page, using JAVA, there would be no reason for people to have such powerful computers on the desktops. Instead they could use the NC or Network Computer which consists of Browser software and very little else. This makes them cheaper than the standard PC and so the cost of new hardware would be that much less.

Control Would Be Increased

Each computer on the standard network could have different software installed and be holding different data which makes for an administrative headache. On an Intranet all the data, and all the software, would be held on an internal website. As that implies one centralised location for everything the system would be much more controllable.

Intranet Project Planning

For most companies the technology needed to create an intranet is already available in the form of computer networks and Browser software. Because of this the temptation is strong to go ahead and create an Intranet without further thought although, as might be guessed, a small amount of extra work at the planning stage will pay dividends. In fact in a study on the subject Cranfield University identified three phases which an Intranet project should go through. These are:

Post It. The replacement of existing paper based systems like telephone directories or price lists.

Use It. Basic interaction with the system such as using in for filling in screen-based expense forms or time sheets.

Sell It. Interactive, i.e. two way, information shared between members of staff or even between staff and customers or suppliers.

The report goes on to suggest that benefits should be achieved from one stage before moving on to the next. A slight problem here is that it can sometimes be difficult to quantify those benefits which obviously makes it difficult to decide if they have been achieved. For that reason an alternative suggestion is to wait until what is known as a critical mass of users has built up before moving on to the next stage. In this context a critical mass is defined as 40% of potential users who should be using the system for at least 10 minutes per session in the first stage (Post It), 15 minutes per session in the second (Use It) and 25 minutes in the third (Sell It).

Even then there are other issues to resolve of which the first is that, as people will only use the system if the information is constantly updated, there must be someone designated to update the information. To be more exact there should be at least one person per department as a system like this is only worth having if the information comes from more than one source and is there to be used by more than one group. If the Intranet is to be used for online training or document management it could even be necessary to employ someone purely to update the Intranet although needless to say the usual cost benefit analysis would have to be done first.

Also on the subject of cost remember that before any benefits are realised by the system some form of staff training would be necessary. This is only to be expected. Before any new system can be used people have to be taught how to use it. Just make sure these training costs are included in the business plan.

Changing the subject slightly there is also one more aspect to this new technology which has probably stimulated more discussion than any other. This is a combination of both Internet and Intranet working together to produce what is now increasingly going by the name of a Virtual Private Network or VPN.

Virtual Private Networks (VPN)

Imagine a web page as seen on a computer through a Browser. Now suppose that web page was stored only in a highly encrypted format so that the Browser needed extra software to read it, and even then only after the right password was entered. If any other Browser had that same software added, and the same key to decode the encryption, it could also read the web page, but no-one else could. For anyone else using the Internet that web page would be unreadable.

Furthermore it would never appear in the search engines so the chances of it being accidentally found amongst the millions of other web pages would be negligible. If such a thing existed it would remain private only to those who knew its URL and who had the key to decode it. That is the basis for the Virtual Private Network.

If company information was stored on an Intranet, which means stored in a manner which could be read by a Browser, then with the addition of an Internet connection that information could be read by any other company office anywhere in the world. All they would need was a similar Browser and their own Internet account. Add encryption to this mix to keep the information confidential and the company would have what amounts to its own private Internet. Any amount of information could be stored in this way and yet from backwoods local office to corporate headquarters that information which companies increasingly rely on would be instantly available. There would be no problems with distances or time zones, nor would there be any delays in collating this information no matter how far flung the enterprise. If need be trading partners or overseas agents could even be added with very little effort. The only difference it would make is that then the system would not be an Intranet, it would be called an Extranet.

This is a truly spectacular vision of what business could be like in the twenty-first century - and yet the technology exists now. All it takes is implementation. To complete the picture for those who want to take it further. Although the company would have its own network, and it would be private, the fact that it uses publicly accessible Internet systems means that it would be a computer generated form of privacy. To put that another way, in the IT industry anything computer generated is said to be virtual hence the name Virtual Private Network. In the jargon the company would have what is known as its own tunnel through the Internet. The idea being that a secure tunnel, or pipe, would exist along which only corporate data would flow, but which would be created using the very public Internet.

A natural extension of this is the idea that employees need not necessarily commute to the office every day. Instead, if they could access the company VPN, they could work from anywhere which is another much talked about concept. This time known as tele-working.

Tele-Working

The whole business of tele-working has now become so confused as to practically defy analysis. On the one hand there are those who claim that soon the entire world will be tele-working, to the detriment of society which is the main point of their claims. Usually these people are journalists or writers who have always worked from home and seem to have no conception that any other kind of work is possible. (Curiously in none of these articles is there an explanation as to who will make the computers everyone is expected to work with, or who will generate the electricity to power them.) Away from all of that, and back in the real world, traditionally there are two types of people who work outside the confines of an office: day extenders and road warriors. Although the Internet has added other categories it would be best to deal with the original two first.

Day Extenders

As the name might suggest these are people who take work home, they extend the working day. Assuming these people also have an Internet connection then current technology means they could link up with the company Intranet and have as much access to information as they would have during normal office hours. This might not make them work any harder, but at least they can expect no hold-ups due to lack of information.

Road Warriors

This could be the sales force, maintenance engineers or company executives; all of whom travel extensively as part of their job. Here, as having access to company information could very probably increase their efficiency, allowing them to connect with the company VPN from a laptop computer could be a worthwhile investment. As ever with any generalised advice this will have to be tailored to suit individual requirements, but it should be considered.

At the same time security should also be considered because it is more than likely that these road warriors will have all access codes and passwords programmed into their laptops. That might make it easy to connect with the VPN from a distant hotel, but if that laptop is ever lost or stolen someone else could access company information just as easily. From a data security point of view it would be like handing over the keys to the company safe. Because of this any organisation which wants to adopt this kind of system should make it clear that whenever a laptop goes missing its owner must immediately inform them so the relevant passwords can be revoked.

Tele-workers

Other than these two types of people, who have always worked away from the office, the Internet has created a third. To be more exact the ease with which information can now be passed from computer to computer has created another kind of worker, but as the mechanism for transmitting that information is usually the Internet in practice it comes to the same thing. In either case it is now possible to be a tele-worker which means somebody who works from home and sends their work to the company via a computer link.

From a technical point of view there is nothing to stop this happening although the fact that such a relatively small number of people are actually doing it would tend to suggest that the reality of the situation is different from the hype. In fact in an effort to maintain the population of rural communities so-called tele-cottages have been set up where all the necessary equipment (computers, modems etc) is available to anyone who walks through the door. Yet despite this the number of people taking advantage of the facilities offered has always disappointed the organisations who sponsored the project. Even where people could have their own facilities at home the response to this new form of working has hardly been overwhelming.

One possible reason for such a lack of enthusiasm could be a simple case of data security. If people are tele-working then the chances are high that confidential company information will be stored on their computer which could be stolen, taking the information with it.

Alternatively that data might not be backed up as regularly as if it was stored in the main office, or, if the computer was used for reasons other than work - which it very likely would be - that same data could be accidentally deleted, altered or infected with a computer virus. (Security experts are so concerned about this that entire seminars are being held on the subject - so far the only advice they have to offer is to stop tele-working.)

Another reason could be that the cost savings tele-working is supposed to bring are not being realised in practice. Here the cost savings are mainly in terms of office space. Those people who work from home will not require their own desk in what could be an expensive town centre office block, or so the theory goes, which means the company will be able to rent less space and so save money. Of course the company will have to pay for all the equipment being installed in the home of the tele-worker, including, possibly, another telephone line dedicated to modem use. Add to that the fact that, by law, the company would still be responsible for ensuring that all health and safety regulations were being followed even by people working from their own home and the drawbacks start to escalate. Not many companies are happy with the thought that they could be prosecuted for negligence because someone trips over an unsecured power cable in their own house.

Despite all of this there are some people who claim practical advantages from tele-working. On the whole these are people whose job requires very little inter-action with other members of staff and whose work is exclusively centred around the production of information in its widest sense. Good examples here would be technical authors producing handbooks for company products or graphic artists. In neither case could these be said to be representative of the work force which probably makes the point: not every job is suitable for tele-working.

And yet the technology most certainly exists to the extent that it has given rise to yet another Internet enabled business, and another buzzword. In this case it is even being talked about as the ultimate evolutionary step for any company, better known as the Virtual Corporation.

Virtual Corporations

Of all the Internet related topics this is probably the strangest to write about. It is definitely the most futuristic. Essentially this is the concept that companies will no longer exist in terms of buildings and offices (bricks and mortar in the jargon). Instead the usual office functions will be scattered, possibly across the globe, from where they are connected together by the Internet.

Technically speaking this is more than possible as it follows on naturally from VPN's and tele-working although why anyone would want to do it is a different matter altogether.

The Case for Virtual Corporations

According to its supporters this can lead to greater operating efficiency as work can be started in one time zone and then at the end of the day it can be transmitted to another site in another time zone where the day is only just beginning. In this way true twenty-four hour a day working can be achieved leading to shorter development cycles and, therefore, products being brought to market faster. This is the approach adopted by one company, the aptly named First Virtual Corporation, although as its business is in developing engineering solutions which are manufactured by other companies on a sub-contract basis it also highlights the weaknesses of the system.

The Case Against Virtual Corporations

For any company where information is the product sold the Internet is ideal. It may even be worthwhile for companies like that turning themselves into virtual corporations. But for those companies where the product is more tangible it is difficult to see where there could be any benefit. Although design companies are an obvious candidate by definition not every company can concentrate purely on design, there have to be other companies who physically manufacture the goods these other companies are designing. For this reason perhaps the best that can be said about virtual corporations is that the idea has yet to be proved in practice.

Even that pre-supposes the concept is worthwhile for information based companies. These virtual offices, or websites, still have to be set up and people still need to be employed to produce whatever information the company is selling so is a virtual corporation any easier, or cheaper, to set up than a more traditional company? If the truth can be better judged by actions rather than words the answer would appear to be no, as one incident makes clear.

As reported in the 'Sunday Times' on 5 April 1998 all the big IT companies (which includes Apple, Microsoft and Texas Instruments) are having problems recruiting British computer programmers to work in America for the very strange reason that British fashion models are so popular in the US. It seems that both need the H-1B visa before they can work there, but as only a limited number are allocated each year the more that are given to fashion models means there are consequently less available for programmers. This has now reached such a point that the companies in Silicon Valley are actively lobbying their government to increase the allocation - by an extra 30,000. Just a story in a Sunday newspaper perhaps, but it does lead to one conclusion:

Despite all talk about tele-working and virtual corporations the big players in the industry apparently still consider that changing the law is an easier option than setting up tele-working facilities. A strange state of affairs for the people selling remote working equipment.

Summary of points worth considering:

♦   Technology allows the company to work in new ways

♦   Does the idea of workers remote from 'the office' appeal

♦   Does information need to be passed around the company's offices in different locations

♦   Teleworking - is it an option

♦   Could your company become a virtual Corporation

Chapter 8

In Conclusion

To sum it all up there is a lot to think about when starting a web project. A lot to think about and a lot to do. So much so that anyone could well feel a company website is beyond their ability when, in fact, the opposite is true. Any reasonably competent manager could take on a web project. They could even see it return a profit for their company. All they have to do is split the project into easy stages. Then complete one stage before moving on to the next.

These different stages are also easy to define, being:

Establish Business Objectives

- Can a business case be made
- Will the site be for advertising only
- Can an e-commerce venture be established
- If so what will be the costs and what will be the expected profit

Decide the Ground Rules

- How will the website fit into the overall marketing strategy
- What will be the impact on current working practices
- Who will need to be involved in development/implementation
- Is the expertise available or will it need to be brought in from outside
- What type of content is needed for the website

Decide the Technical Issues

- Where will the site be hosted
- Will existing hardware/software need to be updated
- How complex will the site be
- Has a security policy been formulated and agreed
- What statistics will be wanted about site traffic

Set a Budget and Agree a Marketing Plan

- Make sure the budget covers the site creation and also maintenance
- The budget might also need to cover staff training
- Advertising the website will also need to be budgeted for

Allocate the Necessary Resources

- Be certain the new orders/enquiries can be handled promptly
- Website advertising and link strategy must be constantly reviewed
- The site must be constantly promoted

Not everyone can be a dot.com millionaire, but they can run a successful website. Many already do. Now is the time to join them.

Appendix A

The History
of the Internet

Of all the world changing events and technologies that can be directly attributed to the cold war perhaps the most unexpected was the creation of the Internet. At the time no-one could foresee how it would develop, now no-one could guess its origins, and yet the Internet was every bit as much a cold war creation as ICBM's or the Berlin Wall.

How it all Began

It began with discussions in the RAND Corporation, a highly influential U.S. think tank, concerning what was then seen as a serious problem: in the event of a nuclear war how could America maintain its communications system? With its defence and research establishments scattered across an entire continent, as the RAND Corporation strategists quickly realised, the U.S. was highly vulnerable to missile attack. Even if its major command centres could be protected nothing could be done about the thousands of miles of telephone cables that stretched between them and carried their orders. Not only that, but the effect of creating alternative, back-up, command centres would be to create just further targets for Soviet missiles. The underlying problem would still be there.

At the height of the cold war, when nuclear attack was seen as more than just a theoretical possibility, this was enough to exercise a lot of minds so that by 1964 the answer was available, in theory at least.

The idea was to create a network of linking computers, each one self-sufficient and each one equal in status to all the others. There would be no central command and, therefore, no single target for the Russians to aim at. Furthermore this network would be designed from the start to assume that the communications system lay in ruins. It would, in other words, not rely on any single telephone line or switching centre. Instead each computer would decide how best to send each message taking whatever route happened to be available. (To be precise each message would be split into smaller packets of information which could be quickly transmitted, via different routes if need be, and then re-assembled at their point of destination, but the principle remains the same.) Additionally each computer would store these messages for later transmission should all routes be blocked.

In this way the RAND Corporation envisaged a network where each computer could transmit its own messages to any other computer, deciding for itself which path to take through the network. If a particular phone line was down due to enemy action, or any other reason, a different phone line to a different computer would be used to by-pass the affected area - once that second computer passed the message on to its intended destination. And with each computer being able to act independently, no matter how badly the country was devastated there would still be some semblance of a communications system and, with it, the control that comes from the ability to issue orders.

Without realising it the RAND Corporation had just designed the Internet as it exists today; a massive collection of computers all passing messages to each other for onward transmission to other computers. No computer has priority over the system nor can anyone know in advance which route the message will take. All that counts is that these messages arrive, and that they most certainly do.

Even so there was still a long way to go before a working version of the Internet appeared. At the time it existed only in theory and in the days when the only available computers were very expensive mainframes turning theory into practice was far from easy.

From a financial point of view alone the project was beyond the reach of the RAND Corporation and so there it could have stayed until, that is, a different organisation entered the picture; another product of the cold war named ARPA.

ARPA

In 1958 the Soviet Union launched Sputnik, the world's first artificial satellite, and sent America into a state of deep shock. Not only had the communist system beat the capitalists in the space race (which was bad enough from a propaganda point of view), but even worse than that it meant Russia was ahead of America in rocket, and therefore missile, technology. In the dark days of the cold war this was something that could never be tolerated. Accordingly the Advanced Project Research Agency (ARPA) was founded whose sole mission was, and still is, to ensure that America maintained its lead in applying new technologies, specifically in defence areas.

It did this by reversing the thinking behind the other military industrial bureaucracies. There the system was that they would invest in new projects only after they could be proven to work. The snag being that with many hi-tech projects the proof of their feasibility would only come after the investment not before as the military demanded; ARPA plugged that loophole.

In fact, with hindsight, ARPA could have been created just to fund the early Internet project so closely did the one match the others' mission statement. Certainly it was no surprise that by December 1969 four computers had been connected to act as individual nodes on what was then known as ARPANET. Nor, given the current popularity of the Internet, would it come as much of a surprise to discover that by 1971 ARPANET had fifteen such nodes, rising to thirty-seven by 1972.

It was then that something strange began to happen. ARPANET was supposed to be for people who needed access to distant computer facilities, instead it was increasingly being used to send personal messages some of which were work related, but most of which was just plain gossip and general chit-chat.

It even reached the point where these people had their own personal accounts on ARPANET computers and their own personal email addresses. The practice was officially frowned on, but still it happened.

What was more News Groups were being established; places where people who shared a common interest could (electronically) discuss their chosen topic. This led almost inevitably to another ARPANET invention, the mailing list whereby the same message could be sent automatically to as many people as subscribed to the list. To this day that is regarded as one of the strengths of the Internet although interestingly, and as a foretaste of things to come, the largest mailing list was for fans of science fiction.

Perhaps because of this the system grew rapidly although mainly, of course, this was as much due to its lack of any centralised command structure. As any computer could be plugged into the net without formality an increasing number were doing exactly that. A good example of this was the accountancy firm of H&R Block who, in 1981, acquired a company allowing computer enthusiasts to make use of the spare capacity on its mainframe during the evening by connecting to it with the newly arrived Personal Computer.

In part this acquisition was so that their clients could file tax returns electronically, but, as history records, that soon became a tiny fraction of the total business. The name of the company was CompuServe.

In fact CompuServe was just one of a great many companies who were now looking to make money from the Internet - of which the most obvious way was to provide an access service to others. These were the so-called ISPs or Internet Service Providers who, for a small monthly fee, offered access to the Internet to businesses and individuals alike. Some were access providers pure and simple while others, like CompuServe or America On Line (AOL), were what is known as content providers. This means they also supplied information (the content of the Internet) to their members such as stock quotes, weather forecasts or even on-line encyclopaedias; anything that would add value to their particular service.

Even so these companies were not wholly responsible for the success of the Internet. That would only happen with the invention of a piece of technology alternatively known as W3, WWW or, to give it its full name, the World Wide Web.

The World Wide Web

Strange to say for an industry so totally dominated by America one of the most important creations was invented in Europe and the man behind it all was British: Tim Berners-Lee.

In 1980 Berners-Lee was working at CERN, the European high-energy research facility based in Geneva, where he wrote a computer program called Enquire Within which was designed to keep track of everything that was happening there. The problem it was designed to solve was that one document could make a reference to the work of another scientist, forcing anyone reading that document to then try and track down information about that scientist, papers written by that scientist or other papers on the same subject written by different scientists. And, to make matters worse, these could all refer to different papers written by different scientists. In other words it was a bureaucratic nightmare which Berners-Lee set out to resolve.

His idea was to use what has since become known as Hypertext: a way of linking information in one document with an entry in another. For example, if a name was mentioned in one document (and assuming that document was on a computer screen) simply clicking on that name would display information about whoever was mentioned as well as providing links to other, related, information which would in turn all have Hypertext links to other documents. In retrospect it sounds simple, good ideas usually do, but at the time it was revolutionary.

Later, with the help of Robert Caillou, Office Computer System Manager, Berners-Lee was able to extend the idea; first on to the local network and then on the Internet as an information retrieval tool. There it made its first appearance in 1991 although by then a Browser had been added.

The Rise of the Browsers

Just as anyone in a library might browse through the book shelves, picking up any book that catches their attention so the same system can apply to the Internet. Assuming the Internet is the library (except the books are in no particular order and the title pages have all been torn off) and websites are the books then the software which allows the website books to be browsed is called, not unnaturally, a Browser. Their appeal lies in the fact that before their arrival searching the Internet involved a multitude of strange, frequently arcane, commands that had to be both learnt and painstakingly entered via the keyboard. After Browsers arrived searching the Internet meant a few clicks of a mouse; so simple anyone could do it.

And anyone did. Before long the term 'surfing the Internet' was adopted to describe jumping from link to link, or web page to web page, just to see what the next site held. As might be expected the term comes from

California where writers looking for something that could evoke excitement with a hint of danger picked on surfing as an appropriate metaphor. With that they could conjure up images of people using their computer surf boards to ride a wave of information quite literally all across the world. That might sound fanciful, but the name stuck and surfing the Internet became increasingly popular.

Soon the call went out for other Browsers to be produced which was famously answered by Mark Andreessen at the National Centre for Supercomputing Applications in Illinois. By February 1993 his team released a Browser called Mosaic which went on to sell over two million copies in the first year, leading Andreessen to found Netscape whose Navigator Browser quickly dominated the market. In fact it was so successful that, at the time, Netscape was seen as a threat to Microsoft itself.

Since the birth of the Personal Computer Microsoft had always supplied the operating system they all ran on, not to mention an increasing amount of related software, but the arrival of the Internet looked set to change all that. As the entire system ran on non-Microsoft software its popularity threatened to undermine the software giant's near monopoly - and its profits. This became even more serious with talk of the so-called NetPC, basically a computer that downloaded its application software from the net every morning and stored its data files back on the Internet rather than a local hard drive. Again this was bad news for Microsoft which explains why the company went from being totally dismissive of all things on-line to producing versions of all its software capable of inter-acting directly with the Internet; followed closely by Internet Explorer, its rival to Netscape Navigator, which first appeared in August 1995

There are those who see this as an attempt by Bill Gates, the Microsoft boss, to retain his domination of the PC world, but whether this be true or not the fact remains that having two such powerful companies in the same market has driven innovation forward to a remarkable degree.

Where it will all end is almost impossible to predict, but there are new technologies and new products coming through which could potentially mean the Internet of the future will be as different to the present as the present is to ARPANET. Even if no-one can say for sure which will succeed by the law of averages some must and so it is worthwhile to consider what these are and how they could shape the future.

The Present and Future

According to those whose business is selling, or reporting on, the Internet the future will be entirely web centred. How far this is true only time will tell, but, nevertheless, it has to be said a lot of money is being invested to make it happen. Currently there are several new technologies all ready to compete for their share of the market.

These are:

Web TV

This is a television and computer hybrid which will allow viewers to either watch TV programmes or, at the press of a button, surf the Internet. With the introduction of digital TV channels this is fast becoming a reality, at least as far as email is concerned. As for websites this is complicated slightly by the fact that many web pages are bigger than the size of the screen. On a computer, with a Windows scroll bar, this is no problem as anyone can always scroll down to see the rest of the page. As this is not possible on a television screen it could well be that the future of web page design lies in making websites smaller and more TV friendly. Needless to say Web TV is the option being promoted most heavily by the television manufacturers.

PCTV

Computer hardware companies take a different line by promoting the PCTV which, as the name suggests, is a computer which can also receive television signals. While this has been possible for some time up until now this has been done by installing an extra circuit board into the computer. This circuit board then receives the TV signal so it can be displayed on the computer monitor.

In the future, however, television signals could be sent out over the Internet and displayed through a Browser. In the place of TV channels there would be TV websites, each one capable of serving even the smallest of minority audiences.

CTI

Another area where different technologies come together is known as CTI or Computer Telephony Integration. In practice this means connecting microphones and camcorders to computers and then using existing Internet technology to send voice and video signals to another computer somewhere else in the world. This second computer would need to be switched on and ready to receive the signal, unlike standard email the message could not be stored and then retrieved later, so in that respect it would function very much like an ordinary telephone.

The difference being that if these two computers were in different countries one very expensive overseas phone call would be traded for two cheap local calls to an Internet Service Provider; potentially a massive saving to anyone who made overseas calls on a regular basis.

Although at present this technology suffers from the poor quality of its signal advances are being made practically on a daily basis to the extent that the technology is already commercially available. As such this, and the so-called video conferencing which is a natural extension of the same principle, looks set to become one of the dominant technologies of the future. (It also explains why all the telecoms companies are so eager to move into the Internet market. Soon it might well be that only local calls are being made which would hit their profits hard unless they had the Internet service business to compensate.)

Push

Less argumentative is the idea of Push technology. Briefly, no matter how much information is stored on the Internet a Browser still has to, in effect, reach out and pull it down the telephone lines. With push technology it will be transmitted automatically whenever a connection is made. Naturally not all the available information can be treated this way, there is just too much of it, so the idea is to have channels of information; in concept very similar to television. One channel will be for sports news, another for business or for entertainment and so on. How successful this is obviously depends in part on the quality of the information being transmitted, but, again, the idea is there and anyone who wants to see it in practice need look no further than Microsoft's Internet Explorer to see it fully implemented.

WAP

Standing for Wireless Application Protocol everyone is expecting this to be the technology of the future (and are already investing billions in it). Simply stated this means the Internet on a portable telephone or any other hand-held device. Again the small size of the screen carries implications for web page design, but other than that the possibilities are limitless. It could well be that a whole new industry will appear, supplying information and services to people on the move. If this is true vast fortunes are waiting for anyone who has a good idea.

Beyond that prediction becomes even harder, especially so as not even the experts can agree. While some are actively planning a ring of communications satellites dedicated solely to Internet traffic others are just as actively predicting its downfall. The need for extra facilities is obvious, just take the current growth rate and extrapolate forward, while at times the predictions of its downfall can be just as obvious. There is just too much out there. Too much that is trivial and far too much that is patently untrue or downright objectionable. As some people are already asking: how long before the system implodes?

While a case can be made for either point of view the truth most probably lies somewhere in between. The Internet will not take over the world nor will it disappear. Instead it will carry on as a medium for business, communication and information. Of course, given that every other prediction about the Internet has been proved wrong, who can say for sure what the future holds. It might grow, it might not; it might change or it might not. About all that can be guaranteed is that it will be impossible to ignore.

Appendix B

How Computers Communicate

Press a button on one computer and a connection can be made with another computer half-way round the world. It might look like magic, but in reality it is nothing more than clever electronics in the modem. Add to that some internationally agreed methods of translating electrical impulses into information, known as protocols, and the job is done. One computer can communicate with another. How that happens in detail is the subject of this chapter.

When it comes to the exact mechanics, or electronics, behind the way computers communicate the first question that needs to be answered is: why would anyone be interested? Other than those people variously described as Geeks, Net Heads, Anoraks, Nerds or the IT Department why would any-one with a life to live want to know how it all works? The fact that it does should be enough for most people which is true, but, unfortunately, only up to a point.

Beyond that everyone needs to know the basics, if only to under-stand some of the more common terms that nowadays no-one can escape.

What follows then is by no means a technical or detailed account of the process involved. Rather, look on it as an overview; a way of learning just enough to take part in the conversations everyone finds themselves having whenever they think about going online, want to go online or are already online. In which case the first port of call should be that box of silicon tricks which makes it all happen: the modem.

The Modem

Long before anything meaningful passes down the telephone line a complex series of signals has already been sent between computer and modem. These are, on the face of it, strange and difficult to follow, but stay with it if only to find out what the flashing lights on the front of the modem mean.

Ready to Send

To begin with the Data Terminal Equipment or DTE (better known as a computer) sends a Ready To Send or RTS signal to the Data Communication Equipment or DCE (better known as a modem). This is sometimes known as a wakeup call and results in the modem sending a Data Carrier Detect or DCD signal to the receiving modem. There then follows a series of signals passed between the two until the communication channel has been established. This process is known as handshaking and helps to explain why, even now, some companies like CompuServe use the symbol of two hands grasping each other to mean being on-line. Of course, after that all it takes is for the second modem to send a Data Set Ready or DSR signal to its computer and wait for the Data Terminal Ready or DTR reply. When that happens the first modem sends a Clear To Send or CTS signal to the computer that started the whole process off and data can then be transmitted. It is as simple as that.

Alternatively, for anyone confused by what the entire Internet industry dubs TLA's which means Three Letter Acronyms, the following diagram should help.

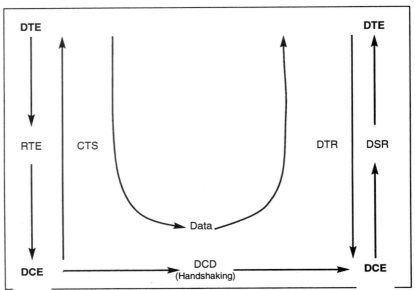

It only looks confusing. Take a second look and everything will soon become obvious.

By way of completeness, these signals are all sent through different pins in the plug which is why the handbooks for all modems and printers carry a pin diagram somewhere in the section on troubleshooting. They are also standardised after the industry leaders met to agree standards for a whole range of peripheral equipment. The Recommended Standard for cable was number 232 which explains that one technical term probably everybody has heard of: RS 232.

Of course, that still leaves the question of exactly how data is transferred from one computer to another; something that is more of a problem than might first appear mainly because the phone lines are analogue while computers are digital. In simple terms this means a telephone signal is constantly changing. To understand that just think of a sine wave as produced on an oscilloscope. The signal might be constant, but it is constantly changing from positive to negative and back again in a series of smooth curves. Computers, on the other hand, can only understand information when it is presented as a string of binary digits so the idea is to map digital output onto an analogue signal.

Without going into technical details this is done by superimposing different frequencies onto the analogue signal (which then becomes known as the carrier wave). Different frequencies can then represent different groups of binary digits in a process which is known as modulation when it is being transmitted and demodulation when it is decoded at the receiving end. Naturally two way communication is achieved by having a single device being capable of both modulation and demodulation, from which the unit takes its name: the modem.

From this it becomes obvious that the more frequencies that can be superimposed on the carrier wave the faster data can be transmitted. Alternatively, to take a different point of view, the more data there is to be transmitted so the more frequencies are needed.

Unfortunately it is only possible to send a limited number of frequencies at the same time, known as the bandwidth, which means communication takes that much longer as the size of the signals steadily increases. Now that pictures, sound and even video sequences are transmitted over the

Internet on a regular basis, and as these all call for massive data files, the amount of available bandwidth is likely to be a problem for some time.

Finally, as the whole process comes down to sending binary digits or bits over a phone line the speed of the system is expressed as Bits Per Second or BPS which is a figure quoted by all the modem manufacturers.

Unfortunately when it comes to data communications there is a lot more involved than just how fast bits can be sent down a phone line. There is also the problem of what those bits mean and how they can be assembled into something intelligible at the far end. Here a whole range of issues need to be addressed and so it might be a good idea to briefly look at the first of these which are the transmission protocols.

Protocols

As in any other walk of life a protocol is just an agreed set of rules to be followed by all concerned. In this case all concerned means Modems which, by following recognised rules of procedure, can communicate with each other. At least, they can if they all follow the same set of rules. This being the software industry there is no such thing as a single standard. Instead many such protocols have been designed, each one just different enough so that there can be no communication between them.

For data transfer to take place both modems must be following the same protocol. Fortunately there are not that many to choose from:

X Modem -   This is the simplest. File names are not automatically sent alongside the data so any software using this system will ask for the name of the file currently being transferred.

Y Modem -   An improved version of X Modem. During transfer file names are automatically added. It is also possible to send more than one file in the same transmission.

Z Modem -   An improvement on Y Modem. If transmission is broken during a file transfer Z modem will transmit only the remainder of the file when the connection has been re-established.

Kermit - Named after the frog this is best described as an alternative to Z Modem.

Fairly obviously these descriptions are simplistic in the extreme, but it would be pointless to go any further. All that really matters is that they exist and form part of the background to data communications. Taking it any further than that would be needlessly technical, especially when other factors also have to be considered. Of these the next, and last, is known as parity.

Parity

As probably everybody knows by now a bit is a binary digit and eight bits make one byte. The chances are everybody also knows that a byte is the standard unit of measurement for all computer files. However, what might not be known is that when every letter, punctuation mark and symbol is given a number so that they can be understood by a computer eight binary digits equates to a decimal number far higher than is needed. All it takes is seven which leaves the eighth either useless or, in the case of data transfer, free to be used as a simple form of error detection.

In fact there are three different forms this can take: odd parity, even parity and no parity. They all follow the same procedure and they can all be explained the same way, but, again, unless both modems are set the same the result will be gibberish.

To explain. A seven digit string of zeroes and ones, which is a number expressed in binary, will obviously have an odd or even number of ones which the eighth - or parity bit - corrects. If odd parity has been selected and there are an odd number of ones then the eighth bit will be zero, but if there are an even number of ones the eighth bit will be one to make the total number odd. In this way the computer can check that every single byte has been received correctly. No digit has been misread during transmission. Needless to say if even parity has been selected the same procedure is followed except that the parity bit is set for even numbers instead of odd.

In practice this is done for more than just each individual byte. Every message is broken down into blocks with every byte checked in this way, known as the horizontal parity, with the final byte being what is known as longitudinal or column parity. In other words if all the bytes were written down one beneath the other the final byte would check each column for parity and correct it for whatever system was being followed.

That might sound complicated, but the procedure is actually very simple as the following diagram shows.

BIT	P	7	6	5	4	3	2	1
	1	0	0	1	1	0	1	0
	0	1	1	0	1	1	0	0
	1	1	0	0	0	0	1	1
			❑			❑		
	1	0	1	0	0	1	0	1

Here bits one through seven, reading right to left, carry the numerical information leaving the eighth or P bit to set the parity. Assuming even parity has been set then the entry in this column makes sure that the total number of binary ones is always even. In exactly the same way the last line makes sure that there are an even number of binary ones in each of the columns with the exception of its parity bit which is there to set its own parity to even. All of which produces a simple yet highly effective form of error detection. (Perhaps obviously no parity means that eighth bit is ignored.)

In the early days of on-line communications modem speed, protocol and parity all had to be set by the individual user which, if it does nothing else, at least shows why Browsers were so amazingly popular. As they do all this automatically data comms (as it was then known) was at last able to move away from the experts and into the hands of mere mortals.

In other words the Internet as it is now could appear although anyone who feels like looking at the settings menu on their Browser will see these same terms in use even today.

It was for that reason they were explained. Anything which helps to make the Internet a more intelligible place has got to be worthwhile in itself quite apart from the way it leads into something even more relevant, namely how the Internet actually works.

How the Internet Works

While everyone knows that the Internet is a gigantic collection of computers all linked together what they forget is that all these computers are different. They operate in different ways, they use different commands and they need different software. How, then, can there be any communication between them?

The answer is Transport Control Protocol/Internet Protocol or, as it is better known, TCP/IP.

TCP/IP

This can best be described as a form of common language all computers speak once the relevant software is installed although this now comes as standard on all computers.

With TCP/IP in place computers can not only talk to each other they can also find each other anywhere in the world. This is because each computer on the Internet is allocated a unique number, in concept exactly like a telephone number complete with area and country codes. While this was all right for computers in practice no human could remember what was of necessity a massive string of numbers just to identify a particular machine. They, we, needed something more memorable and so it was the DNS or Domain Name System came into being.

Basically this is a way of mapping (relatively) easily remembered names, like WWW.COMPANYNAME.CO.UK, onto the appropriate number. There is a bit more to it than that as there is no such thing as a central directory of all numbers. (If there was that would create a single point of failure or a highly vulnerable target which the original designers of the Internet were chiefly concerned with avoiding.) Instead the name is broken down into various sub-directories, each with their own backup sites, so that in the example above COMPANYNAME would be the name of the computer found in one directory which would be a sub-set of the directory .CO. which itself would be a sub-set of the directory .UK.

From all of this it soon becomes obvious how the Internet works. Someone sitting in front of a computer enters a web address into their Browser. The computer then searches one directory which points it to another, which points it to a third until the unique number (the IP address) for that particular name is found and a connection is made. For good measure the Browser also stores that number so the next time the equivalent name is entered it can go straight there without the need for a search. How simple can it get?

And the answer is, not quite that simple. For one thing TCP/IP has no idea where the Domain Name Servers are or what to ask for when it finds them. For that an entirely different protocol is used. Once that was SLIP (Serial Line Interface Protocol) although, despite being still supported by even the latest version Browsers, that has since been superseded by PPP (Point to Point Protocol).

The advantage of using PPP is that it supports security features known as PAP and CHAP. PAP is Password Authentication Protocol which allows a password to be sent over the Internet to confirm a caller's identity before access to a particular system is granted.

A more secure method is CHAP (Challenge Handshake Authentication Protocol). Here no password is sent which cuts out the risk of it being intercepted. Instead the calling computer sends an identifier and a challenge value. The receiving computer then combines these two values with the password to create a third value which is returned to the calling computer. The calling computer then decodes this to find the original value. If the two values match then not only is the password authenticated, but both computers also have their identities confirmed which reduces the risk of a hacker attack known as IP Spoofing (one computer pretending to be another as a way of stealing confidential information).

After that comes the problem of the World Wide Web which TCP/IP was never designed to cope with. So, once again, another protocol is needed. In this case Hypertext Transfer Protocol or HTTP. With that anyone can surf the net without even knowing what has to happen before they can do it. To be more accurate anyone can surf the Internet providing they have an Internet connection which is not quite as straightforward as it sounds. There are, in fact, many different ways for a company to be connected to the Internet. Somewhat naturally they vary both in cost and complexity, but they should all be understood if only to know what the options are.

Internet Connections

The simplest of these is known as a dial-up connection which describes it exactly. Software installed on a computer instructs a modem, also connected to the same computer, to dial the number of an Internet Service Provider; a connection is made, an account number is automatically sent to the ISP and the web surfing can begin once that is verified. Literally it is as simple as that.

Even so now might be a good time to deal with some of the jargon surrounding the issue. In this case it concerns something known as a PoP, or to be more accurate a local PoP, which all service providers are supposed to have. This particular acronym actually stands for Point of Presence, or local Point of Presence, and means the service provider has offices close by which the modem calls to make an Internet connection so subscribers only have to pay for a local phone call.

An alternative to this is a Virtual Point of Presence which is just a jargon-laden way of saying the modem dials the kind of number which charges a local call rate no matter where in the country the call comes from. The modem can, of course, also dial a toll free number just as easily which is how the ISPs can now offer free access to the Internet.

If all a company wants a website for is to advertise its name or products on the Internet a dial-up connection is perfectly adequate as the website itself could be stored on a computer owned by the service provider or even the web design agency (in the jargon they would host the website). If this is done the company itself could then concentrate on such things as searching the Internet or sending email, always assuming such things were part of the corporate plan for Internet use.

However, as simple as it is a dial up connection can sometimes be a costly option, particularly if the service is used extensively either by one individual spending hours on-line or by many people who collectively spend a long time online. Under these circumstances the cost of the phone call itself becomes significant and leased lines start to be viable. As a general rule of thumb a total of five hours on-line per day is considered to be the break even point. After that even a local phone call becomes an expensive luxury and other options should be considered.

Options

Of these the first is the straightforward leased line, of which no more need be said. The second option, however, is a piece of technology known as ISDN or Integrated Services Digital Network. Without going into technical details this is really no more than a type of telephone line capable of carrying the kind of digital signals a computer can understand. It has the advantage of much faster data transfer than the standard copper cable which, obviously, makes for faster downloads from the Internet. Additionally if the need arises two separate ISDN cables can be used simultaneously to double the transfer rate; something that could be important if large files, like video clips for example, are to be transferred over the system.

Going on from there another way of connecting to the Internet is known as dedicated access. This calls for a permanent leased line to the ISP plus what is known as a port into the Internet, basically a way of plugging the corporate computer system directly into the Internet itself which can be provided by the ISP. Any company whose computers are connected together into a network (better known as a LAN or Local Area Network) would find this invaluable as anyone on that network would have immediate access to the Internet through a single connection, assuming every computer was configured to understand and use TCP/IP.

The last option, an ISP offering free access is, surprisingly, the hardest to calculate as that calculation must include whatever monthly fee the ISP will charge plus the possible extra phone line needed to maintain that Internet connection all day long. (The quality of service being offered by the ISP should also be taken into account)

By way of completeness it should also be mentioned that there are many places where a website could be stored or, to put that into Internet jargon, where the website could be hosted. In no particular order these are:

The ISP

While the Internet Service Provider could store a website on one of its own computers it could equally allow a company computer holding the website to be installed on its premises. This computer would, in turn, be connected both to the company by leased line and also to the

Internet. Under this system it is the ISP who has the problem of maintaining the website and computer while all the company has to do is pay for the service.

Third Party

The website could equally be hosted by a third party company which could be either the web design agency offering an extra service or a company which specialises in website hosting.

Company Computers

As the name implies the company who owns the website stores it on one of its computers in its own premises. The Internet connection then runs from that computer to the ISP, most usually by leased line as this option is for the more complex sites. Furthermore permanent access to the Internet would be necessary so the website could be viewed twenty-four hours a day.

For the user, then, nothing could be simpler, but for the manager who has to justify its use life is not nearly so kind. For them a whole range of issues have to be considered and new types of consultant or contractor have to be dealt with. Some will be highly professional and talented, but, in such a relatively young industry, others will be cowboys intent only on baffling the uninformed with all the latest buzz words, acronyms and jargon.

Against that there can only be one line of defence: knowledge. With that the right decisions can be taken, the right people consulted and the right questions asked. In short, with that the Internet will become a useful, productive, tool where money can be earned not wasted. All it takes is understanding.

Appendix C

Web Software

Despite appearances a website is not a single piece of software. Rather it is a collection of computer programs which together make up the website. From this it follows that to understand how a website can be constructed calls for a working knowledge of the software (aka the computer programs). To do that, read on.

If it has done nothing else the Internet has created a whole new branch of the software industry dedicated to supplying the ever more sophisticated needs of its users. In some ways this is only natural. From a text-only system the Internet has rapidly changed into a transmission medium capable of supporting sound, pictures and even video each with their own processing requirements which, while they might make it a friendlier place to visit, have done nothing to make it any more comprehensible.

All of a sudden there are yet more strange-sounding names, acronyms and initials to be mastered and yet it has to be done. How else can a raw beginner (a newbie in net-speak) ever hope to understand the basics of creating a website? And without that understanding how can they ever hope to do business with the people who create those websites?

Fortunately there are only a few such pieces of software and they can be explained very easily, in concept at least. At the end of this no-one will be able to write their own computer programs, but they will be able to understand those who do which has got to be a major plus. And if anyone doubts that imagine trying to control a project without the faintest idea of what everyone else is talking about.

Better yet imagine having to negotiate with outside contractors, and pay their bills, without knowing whether their work is at the rocket science level or so easy the proverbial seven year old could do it.

In other words it has to be done, but, to look on the bright side, in this case at least a little learning can go a long way. To prove that perhaps the best place to start is not with web software, but with the software needed to read web pages: the Browser.

Browsers

A Browser is a piece of software that everybody needs if they want to surf the Internet for useful or interesting websites. Web pages are designed to be read by Browsers and Browsers are designed to read web pages. Fortunately, acquiring a Browser is slightly easier than catching the common cold. They are everywhere. Most computers now come with one pre-installed. A great many CD-ROMs are now designed to be read like a website and so include a Browser which can be installed onto a computer's hard drive and ISPs give them away free to anyone who signs up for their service. There is nothing difficult about acquiring a Browser.

There is also nothing difficult about using one. Just click on the icon of whatever ISP is being used and the Browser will launch itself automatically. After that all it takes is to enter the address of a particular website, click on go, and the job is done. Browsers are a rare example of software which truly is user-friendly.

Email Readers

These are used both to read email and to send it. For this reason anyone who wants to use the Internet for the sending and receiving of email will need a reader. Once again, though, there is nothing difficult about acquiring one. When Browsers are installed they also come with an option to install an email reader and ISPs will also offer one to anybody who signs up to their service.

Even so, now might be a good time to dispel some of the myths surrounding email. Of these the first is that emails can only be read on-line. In fact when a message is sent to an individual, or company, the ISP stores it until the person concerned next goes on-line. Then the messages are transferred to that person's computer where they can be read at any time. Think of these email messages as just another word processed document that can be opened at will and it should make sense. In fact many people go on-line just long enough to collect their mail and then quit the Internet, saving the actual reading of their email until later.

An email can also be written off-line. The email software can store any number of messages written in advance of going on-line so that they can be sent later. Alternatively, an urgent message, once composed, can be sent immediately although here the email software will connect itself to the Internet, send the message and then promptly end the Internet session.

Both the sending and receiving of email should take no more than a few sec-onds of on-line time. That is what makes email so cheap and so convenient.

HTML

As the name probably makes obvious Hypertext Markup Language is what everybody uses to create web pages. All of which makes it sound extremely complicated when, in fact, the opposite is true. Anyone who could use a word processor in the days before Windows and its point and click operations can create a basic web page using HTML.

At the heart of the system are what are known as tags which are basically formatting instructions to tell the Browser how to display whatever is between a particular pair of tags. For example:

This point is important

By convention tags are enclosed in <> symbols which are the less than and greater than signs found on any keyboard. In this case the <b> tag means show everything in bold face until the second tag is reached. Again by convention the second tag includes the forward slash, '/', so that </b> means stop using bold face and revert to standard text. After that all it takes is to know what the different tags mean and anyone can program in HTML.

Nothing could be more straightforward. In fact this is exactly the same technique as was used to format text on the pre-Windows word processors which explains the comment made earlier. Not only that, but, as a sign of how pervasive the Internet has become, all modern word processors and Desktop Publishing (DTP) packages include the facility to create web pages as standard. All anyone has to do is design the page on screen then click on the menu option for HTML and the job is done. Alternatively there are now any number of specialist software packages available which are designed to do no more than to create web pages, complete with all manner of fancy special effects. It gets easier as time goes by.

In fairness to the people who create web pages for a living it has to be said there is more to it than that. Just as Desktop Publishing or word-processing brought document creation to the masses so the comments made then apply every bit as much to web creation. The software gave everybody the ability to do it, but not the talent to do it properly. There is still a world of difference between a professionally created document or web page and that produced by an amateur who happens to have the right software - and it shows. For one thing there is the question of managing the links to other web pages.

For example a typical website might consist of an opening screen complete with company logo and the option to link web surfers with, say, company information, product information, a screen for placing an order and links to other related sites. Each one of these is a web page in its own right and must include the facility for surfers to navigate forward and backwards between the relevant pages or even jump from one to the other. If not someone who reads the product information might find the business of placing an order on-line so complicated as to be not worth the bother. In which case what point is there in having a website in the first place?

So, while web creation is not the exclusive domain of professionals, there is still a lot to consider. Even so, supposing the job is left to the experts, there are many other points to be aware of. Sometimes these experts can have their own agendas far removed from the best interests of the company paying the bills, but to explain that first a little bit of history has to be understood.

The History of HTML

In 1986 the International Organisation for Standardisation released ISO 8879 entitled 'Information Processing - Text and Office Systems - Standard Generalised Markup Language (SGML)'. Although this defined a standard for the first time nothing much happened after that, mainly because no-one knew what to do with it. Then Tim Berners-Lee invented the World Wide Web and suddenly the demand was there.

Everybody wanted hypertext documents. More than that everybody wanted to produce software that would create hypertext documents, if only so they could control the standard.

In the software industry standards (the standard or industry accepted way of doing something that all other software manufacturers must conform to) is just about the ultimate prize. Should one company create a standard, known as a de facto standard in that every other company must follow it despite it never being ratified by a standards committee, then the financial rewards can be truly spectacular. Not only does it have the prestige of being the mar-ket leader which can be easily translated into sales, but, if the technology can be patented or copyrighted in some way, then every other company in the business will have to buy a licence to use it before they can even begin to compete. A lucrative affair in its own right made even more so by the fact that whoever controls the standard sets the standard. Practically speaking that means they can change it whenever they like, forcing the consumer to buy new software and the rest of the industry to buy new licences.

Standards, and their control, is therefore an important issue which helps to explain why the W3 Consortium was set up in 1994 to oversee the process, at least as far as the Internet was concerned. Theoretically any web page written to conform to the W3 standard can be read by any Browser no matter where it comes from.

If only life was that simple.

With such massive profits at stake the companies concerned are all pushing ahead with advancements to their own Browsers which, they hope, will become so popular that the W3 Consortium will have no choice but to include it in their next official standard release. A good business practice it might be, but along the way all it really produces is confusion the outcome of which is that some websites which include these new features are unreadable by other Browsers.

On a practical basis, then, before anyone is given the go-ahead to design a web page they should be made to state explicitly, and in writing, either that it will incorporate only those features officially approved by the W3 Consortium or if not they must provide a list of all Browsers that will support it. In this case they should also give the version number of each

Browser and, just as importantly, the date it was released. That way the company who expects the website to work for them, and are paying for it, can make their own decisions about the size of the market being reached - or being excluded. For example if a feature is supported by the latest version of Microsoft Internet Explorer the question is how many people are likely to be still using an earlier version which can only be decided when the date of its release is known. Not everyone downloads the latest version immediately it becomes available. A frequently recommended practice is to wait until the early adopters find the bugs and the software company fixes them. Then, when the package is known to be stable and safe, the upgrade can be performed without undue hazard.

Also, remember how the software industry works. What is leading edge today is standard technology tomorrow and almost obsolete the day after (and practically on that time scale). For the web design agencies this creates a tremendous pressure to be constantly working at the leading edge so that when it becomes standard technology they already have the experience and expertise in its use which they can then sell to other clients.

Of course for those first few clients using that leading edge technology this has several implications:

◆   Delivery could be delayed. If a system has to be learnt before it can be implemented no-one can be sure how long it will take.

◆   The final product could be flawed. If a system is new no-one can be certain it will work flawlessly, not without extensive testing leading to further delays. Alternatively the website could go live with its faults still undiscovered and still in place making the whole exercise useless.

◆   The site could be invisible to some users. If a Browser cannot support the features of a particular website it will be unable to read some or all of that website.

While a reputable design agency will make their client aware of all this not every agency is reputable and so the questions should be asked. At the very least the agency should be able to explain the potential shortcomings of each and every feature included in a proposed website.

Better yet should there be even the slightest hint of a problem the onus should be on the design agency to justify that particular feature. Remember, the only people who score points for having fancy web pages are the web design agencies. Everyone else can make do with bog standard technology. And if the agency cannot create a good looking site with the tremendous variety of features which already exists as standard then find an agency that can.

Next, as if the entire business was not already over-complicated, there are yet more ways in which the waters can be muddied even further. In this case the culprit is a particular piece of software generally referred to as a plug-in.

Plug-Ins

Essentially these are extra programs that can be installed and used as part of a Browser i.e. they plug into it. Typically these would provide extra facilities like the ability to handle sound files or advanced graphics. What this means in practice is that, should a web page incorporate sound as well as text, the relevant plug-in will be needed before it can be read by any Browser and the sound played through the computer's own speakers.

Here the word 'relevant' means the matching plug-in to whatever piece of software was used to create that particular sound effect on the web page. Plug-ins come in sets of two; one is sold to the web designers to create a particular effect and the other is given away free to anyone with a Browser so they can see or hear that effect on their own computers.

Needless to say, this being the computer industry, there are a lot of plug-ins to choose from - and there is no such thing as compatibility. Every one of these special effects needs its own plug-in installed on the Browser. Some sites get around this by including a link to the plug-in manufacturer's home page where the relevant piece of software can be downloaded immediately, but, that apart, there is nothing else that can be done. Without the right plug-in the effect is unreadable.

It has to be said that some of these special effects can do wonders for a web page and really make it stand out from the crowd. It is even possible that some people will turn to that web page just to see it for themselves once the word spreads so there are good reasons for using them, naturally.

However, on the basis that the web designers will be more than ready to sing the praises of these things, perhaps it might be a better idea to concentrate on the down side.

First, and most obvious, is the fact that a special plug-in has to be installed on each individual Browser. As these are given away free that might not seem too much of a problem which would be a fair point if there were only one or two on the market. Unfortunately the number available is steadily increasing to the point where not even the most dedicated web surfer could hold them all. For those less dedicated, or still holding on to the notion that the computer is a business tool and the space on its hard drive should be reserved for business information, that applies even more so.

Also while these plug-ins are given away without charge it would be wrong to say there were no costs involved. All the manufacturers do is set up a website where anyone who wants it can download their particular merchandise - except the phone call might still have to be paid for. All of which explains why not everybody has even the most popular of plug-ins; they have better things to do with their on-line time and better ways of spending their money, especially as the size of these files means a long download. Stripped of its jargon that means waiting for what will seem like an eternity as some form of graphical display measures how much of that file has been received - and how much is still to come.

It therefore follows that plug-ins should be treated with caution. While they can greatly enhance a website, and in so doing greatly increase its value as a marketing tool, they do have their drawbacks as the extra cost of including them will be wasted if not everyone can read them. Because of this there can be no hard and fast rules about their use. Each case has to be judged entirely on its own merits which can only be done when a variety of factors are taken into consideration.

These are:

♦ How well known is it. An obscure plug-in will have very few users.

♦ How popular is it. All the manufacturers have statistics about the number of downloads from their site. These should be consulted when assessing the total number of people who will have that particular plug-in.

◆ How necessary is it. Is that particular effect so vital the site will be useless without it. If not why have it?

◆ Are there alternatives. Can a similar effect be achieved some other way either by using a more popular plug-in or by using more standardised methods.

◆ Who will see it. A highly technical, computer literate, user is more likely to have these plug-ins already installed. On the other hand a more general user might not even know what a plug-in is. That being the case consider who is likely to visit the website and take the decision accordingly.

Other than that there is very little advice that can be given. The situation is just too dynamic for even generalised rules quite apart from the fact that as each website and each plug-in are both in some way unique the number of permutations is, for all practical purposes, infinite.

That being the case ask the questions, take an informed decision - and then go on to consider the next piece of web software.

CGI

This is yet another acronym which actually stands for Common Gateway Interface. Basically this is nothing more than a way of embedding small programs in the website to do things like counting the number of visitors or adding a form so that visitors can send a message to the company who owns the site. To an experienced programmer it is far from difficult (and a lot of such programs can be downloaded off the Internet itself) although, naturally, they do add an extra level of complexity to any website.

Active Content - Java and Activex

In 1994 the computer company Sun Microsystems scrapped an unsuccessful programming language called Oak which it had developed to allow various items of consumer electronics to communicate with each other. However with the Internet rapidly increasing in popularity Sun co-founder Bill Joy saw that with a few modifications Oak could become a programming environment for the World Wide Web. Accordingly Sun continued to fund the project and in January 1995 the company was able to release its new Internet programming language now named Java (after a type of coffee not the island west of Krakatoa).

The strength of Java lies in its platform independence. What this means is that where most software is designed to run on a particular type of computer like the Windows PC and then has to be redesigned to run on the Apple computer, for example, Java can run on both without modification. It does this by creating what is known as a Virtual Machine or VM inside each computer which inter-acts with that computer's operating system and translates the program itself into something the computer can understand. This program or applet (pronounced app-let to signify it is a mini-application) is then loaded into the Virtual Machine where it does whatever job the designer intended it to do.

Obviously from the point of view of the Internet which consists of every type of computer imaginable this was ideal. A program written in Java could be stored on a web page and then transferred to any user regardless of what computer they were using. With Java web pages need no longer be static, which is to say composed only of text and fixed images, now text could be made to move around the screen as could graphics - hence the name active content. In fact anything could be done to give websites the fascinating variety of content that now exists. The only limit was imagination.

To be more down to earth the only limit was how fast web developers would adopt this new system which was hampered in no small part when Microsoft introduced its rival ActiveX technology. Similar in concept to Java ActiveX also allowed applets to be downloaded from web pages although in the Microsoft version there was no Virtual Machine for them to work with. Instead each tiny program was allowed free access to the operating system of the host computer, again to do whatever the designer intended it to do.

In defence of its new product Microsoft claimed that without the Virtual Machine adding an extra layer of commands to slow the system down their ActiveX components worked that much faster than Java. And it has to be admitted Java applets are slow to download and to run, but the implications of letting these programs issue commands directly to the operating system are almost beyond belief. (For more see the chapter on security.) Even so from the point of view of the general user neither system presents any major problems. Any Browser will support both Java and ActiveX.

Finally there is one last piece of software which needs to be taken into consideration either when a website is being designed or being used. This goes by the name of Cookies.

Cookies

In American homes, or so the story goes, when visitors arrive they are given a cookie which in Britain would be a biscuit. This philosophy has now been extended to the Internet. Whenever a visitor, better known as a Browser, arrives at certain sites a cookie is sent down the line and saves itself to the local computer's hard disk.

There is nothing mysterious or dangerous about this. All it means is that there are certain sites which ask for personal or company details before they allow access to the website proper. This can be either to collect marketing information, visitor statistics or even to restrict access to those sites offering a premium rate service which could be anything from stock quotes to hard core pornography. Anything is possible, but the point is, having entered those details once, it would be tedious beyond belief if a regular user had to constantly enter those same details every time they visited the site. In other words what was wanted was a system whereby the details could be entered only once and then transmitted automatically every time the website was re-visited - otherwise known as a cookie.

A cookie is nothing more than a very small text file containing whatever information that particular website needs to allow the user access. They are not dangerous, they cannot harm the computer in any way and they even come complete with an expiry date. All they do is automate what would otherwise be a time consuming, and annoying, operation.

Obviously from the point of view of a web designer they can be a valuable tool which is why they are mentioned here, but, that apart, there is nothing to think about. If a particular website would benefit from being able to create its own cookies the web designer will mention it, if not they are just a curiosity of Internet life which can for the most part be safely ignored.

Appendix D

Using and Searching the Internet

For most people using the Internet means finding information or entertainment in a variety of different web pages. While this constitutes the bulk of all Internet traffic there are other options available such as email, FTP and Usenet each one of which must be dealt with separately.

That being the case the best place to start would be with the biggest and arguably the most important: searching the Internet. Unfortunately before any kind of sense can be made of the various search techniques, or of the search engines themselves, anyone must have at least a working knowledge of something known as Boolean Logic.

Boolean Logic

This was first created by an English mathematician named George Boole in 1847 and yet, in one of the strange quirks of the computer industry, is now used in everything from circuit design to searching the Internet. In essence Boole developed a system for reducing complex questions into simple yes or no answers by using what are known as truth tables, sometimes called gates.

Although these truth tables or gates can take several forms the three that are relevant to Internet searches are AND, OR and NOT. Each one operates differently.

and

This produces an output only if two specified conditions are met. For example if a search was made on the words 'Economic' AND 'Policy' the truth table would be as follows:

1st Condition (Economic)	2nd Condition (Policy)	Output
NO	NO	NO
YES	NO	NO
NO	YES	NO
YES	YES	YES

Only if both words were found on the same website would a match be returned.

or

This produces an output if either specified condition is met. In the same example as above the truth table would be:

1st Condition (Economic)	2nd Condition (Policy)	Output
NO	NO	NO
YES	NO	YES
NO	YES	YES
YES	YES	YES

If either word is found on a website a match would be returned.

not

This returns an output only if a specified condition is not met. To continue the above example if a search was made on the words 'Economic' NOT 'Policy' the truth table would be:

1st Condition (Economic)	2nd Condition (Policy)	Output
YES	YES	NO
NO	YES	NO
YES	NO	YES
NO	NO	NO

Only websites which contain the word 'Economic' but do not contain the word 'Policy' will be returned.

In electronics the output from one set of gates can become the input to others to produce complex switching arrangements which forms the basis of the computer microchip itself. Away from that it is by combining these various logical operators (as AND, OR and NOT are known) that highly precise Internet searches can be conducted, as will soon become clear.

Search Engines

As all search engines are different they all operate in slightly different ways. The good news is that the same search techniques can be applied to them all, but, as might be expected, each one is a variation around the same theme. To make it even worse not all search engines actually search the Internet, some are what is known as web directories. Then, just to confuse the picture even more some engines do keyword searches while others are concept based.

Put that all together and it becomes obvious why some people stop using the Internet - and those that still do help to earn vast profits for the ISPs and telecoms companies. With tens of millions of websites and very little idea of how to search through them it is usually at this point that people start to give up; when a simple search produces several hundred thousand matches none of which appear relevant.

And yet this could so easily be changed. All it takes is a basic understanding of the terms used and the application of a few simple techniques. First, what do the terms mean.

Web Directories

In concept these are identical to any other directory, or even the Yellow Pages. Websites are grouped into categories and those categories are listed alphabetically to make searching the Internet a simple matter of looking up the right category. With web directories the problem is knowing what category to look under.

Search Engines

These actually do search every website on the Internet using what are known as software agents which can also have a variety of other names.

Sometimes they can be called Web Robots or just Robots; they can also be called Bots, Web Crawlers because they crawl all over the web or, finally, they can be called after the creature that traditionally crawls over webs: Spiders. Why they should have so many names is beyond even the experts, but they do at least all work in the same way.

Every website is searched and the content found there indexed according to the title of that website, any words found between the <META> tags and also any other words found in the text. For good measure the links pointing to a particular website can also be analysed as the words surrounding that link can help to describe the website the link points to. All search engines work slightly differently; some give a higher preference to words found within the text of a website, others concentrate on the words within the <META> tags. In the end, though, they all produce a list of indexed words. It is these indexed words that are then searched to find a match for any word entered into the search engine by anyone using the service. For good measure these same web robots continually re-visit each website both to confirm it still exists and to make a note of any alterations which could affect how it was indexed.

Finally, there are some search engines that take any search term entered into them and pass it on to a variety of other search engines. The results from all these search engines are then displayed.

There are, then, many different ways in which a search engine can operate. And far too many search engines to list. That being the case the best advice is to find a few that seem to match any personal preferences and use them. It is always a good idea to use more than one search engine when looking for information as their different ways of working means they will always produce a slightly different list of websites.

It is also easy to find search engines on the Internet. Just do a search using the term "search engine".

Keywords

This is a system employed by search engines to supply a list of websites matching the criteria entered by a user. As the name implies it is a straightforward word match. If the word entered by a user is found on a website its URL is added to the list of results.

The problem with this method is that words can frequently have more than one meaning which the search engines cannot differentiate between. For example a search on the word 'heart' would produce a list of both medical and romantic websites. The search engine would also ignore any sites where this word was not included so, in the above example, the word 'cardiac' would not be considered a match.

Keywords can also find it difficult to distinguish between words that are the same, but which have a different stem. For example Big, Bigger and Biggest all mean the same thing, but not to a search engine.

Concept Based Searches

Here an attempt is made to search the Internet according to the concept represented by a word rather than the word itself. In this way a term like heart attack would also produce a match against the term cardiac arrest. Unfortunately this method calls for some highly sophisticated programming known as Artificial Intelligence (AI) which is a science still very much in its infancy. The results can therefore be sometimes wildly inaccurate. T

his system also calls for a great many words to be entered into the search engine so their context can be judged. For example is the word 'heart' being used in its medical or romantic sense. If the next word was 'flowers' this would give a different result than if the next word was 'artery'.

Although all of this should be understood, if only so the right search engine can be chosen, it is still of very little help when it comes to the business of actually searching the Internet. For that a different set of techniques are needed which, finally, makes use of the previously mentioned Boolean logic.

Search Techniques

There is nothing difficult, or particularly complex, about searching the Internet. No special skills are required nor does it take years of practice, major qualifications or an affinity with all things technological. In short, anyone can do it (repeat anyone). Like many other apparently complex tasks the major hurdle, in this case the only hurdle, is the shock of the new. Once that is overcome it all comes down to little more than common sense. The search engines even have a sign saying 'Enter search term here'; how easy can it get?

Incidentally, finding a search engine on the Internet is also easy as they have a URL the same as any other website. Enter that into a Browser, wait for the page to load and the searching can begin.

As already mentioned the basis of any search involves Boolean logic, but, just to make it even easier, this is also supplemented by a few other commands which can be used in any combination to make possible extremely precise searches. these are:

Proximal Locators

A proximal locator is simply a means of telling a search engine to look for one word close to, or in the proximity of, another. Depending entirely on the search engine this can take the form of NEAR (As in scotch NEAR whiskey) which means the two words must be within ten words of each other to record a match.   Another proximal locator is the term FOLLOWED BY which is self-explanatory although some engines use the term ADJ for Adjacent.

Quotation Marks

If the search criteria is a phrase rather than a word enclosing this in quotation marks ("") means websites will only be returned if that phrase appears instead of the individual words. For example the search criteria of United States will include every website which includes the word United plus every website which includes the word States. (In many search engines the default operator is OR.) However, if the search term "United States" was entered only those websites which mentioned America would be returned.

Capital Letters

If capital letters are used anywhere in a search expression, like the first letter in a name, the search will match only those websites which likewise use those capital letters. Alternatively if a word is entered without the use of capitals the search will match websites where that word appears regardless of capitalisation.

Stop Word

There is also something known as a stop word which is really just the kind of small word that would never be the subject of a search like 'the', 'a', 'an' or 'is'. The search engines ignore these so do the same otherwise there could be no space left to enter an extra search term.

Now comes the business of actually searching the Internet.

Search Results

Whenever a name is entered into a search engine there will be one of two possible results, either zero matches will be returned or the total will run into hundreds of thousands. If no matches are returned, which happens surprisingly often, the only solution is to enter a different word and try again. Think up something else that means the same then repeat the process until result number two is obtained.

When that happens there will be too many matches which is where the Boolean operators come into their own. To use them start by thinking of a second search word which qualifies the first and enter them both, with the appropriate logical operator naturally.

For example if the word grass was entered the search would return a list of websites ranging from gardening to drugs (slang terms can also be searched for). So, to narrow the field, enter a search like grass AND lawn which means both words must be present on a website. Unfortunately as all it takes for a website to be included in the search results is some comment on the web page about how this is not the type of grass likely to be found on a lawn this will still return far too many matches, but by looking at the websites to see what they contain the search can be refined further.

In this case to something like grass AND lawn NOT music (some sites will be for blue grass music which will be excluded by the NOT operator). Then take it further with another search like grass AND lawn NOT music NOT cooking (specifically Thai lemon grass recipes for those who were wondering). This will reduce the list of websites to something more manageable although as it will still run into tens of thousands other refinements may need to be added.

Even without that the principle involved can be clearly seen; making other searches just more of the same. As with everything else in life better results will come with practice, but it takes nothing more than that. Practice and a small amount of knowledge is all anybody needs to search the Internet with ease.

With so many search engines in existence it is impossible to list the characteristics of each one. For example, in some cases the Boolean operators AND and NOT can be replaced by the symbols + and - but just to list those search engines that do and those that do not would take another book all by itself, especially as all the other differences would have to be mentioned. Because of that the best advice that can be given is to use the button on the search engine marked hints or tips. As this gives information exclusively relevant to that particular search engine it has to be the best place to look.

Unfortunately in the early stages of any search the result always seems to be a massive list of websites very few of which have any relevance to the search in question - and yet the search engine insists they are all ranked in order of relevancy. Despite appearances this apparent contradiction has nothing to do with the efficiency, or otherwise, of the search. Instead it is caused entirely by the way search engines assign that relevancy which should be explained if only to make sense of the results obtained.

Relevancy Rankings

To begin with most engines use what is known as search term frequency. This means the more often a word being searched for appears on a particular web page the more relevant that particular page is assumed to be. As simplistic as that sounds it does work although there are some engines which take that one step further and also consider the position of the search word within a page. If the word appears at the top, or close to the top, of the page then it is more likely that the page in question concerns the subject being searched for.

Again that might appear overly simplistic, or even primitive, but it can be proved to work. Should anyone doubt that consider how often the word 'Internet' appears in this book, and how close the word is to the top of the very first page. If this book was a website and the search word was 'Internet' this book would achieve a very high relevancy rating indeed.

Links

Even so a third factor is involved, namely the number of links a site has. The greater the number of links the higher the relevancy. This is justified on the grounds that if other people think the site is important enough to link with it then the search engine is prepared to accept their judgement. (Genuinely, that is the argument put forward.)

Of course the practical point to all of this is that in the initial stages of a search the relevancy ranking should be ignored. As already mentioned words can have multiple meanings and sites can have hundreds of links all of which will affect the rankings until the search terms are refined. A website listed as number 200 or even 200,000 could be the site wanted, but without looking no-one would ever know. Therefore look. Do more than just consider the top ten or twenty websites in any list, pick a few more at random and have a look at them. Even if they are still irrelevant just by looking at a greater range and seeing what they have in common will help to determine what should be included or excluded from the next search. In other words it is worth doing.

Error Codes

Even if all it produces is an error code it is still worth doing for the times when it leads to a valid website. As for those error codes they will be encountered by anybody simply because the Internet is constantly changing; websites might change their address and others might no longer exist. Add connection problems and it soon becomes obvious why these error messages are needed. They give valuable information to Internet users, or, rather, they can when the Internet user knows what these error codes mean. For that, read on.

Error code

301   The requested resource has been permanently moved to a new URL. (Usually this is accompanied by the new location and the Browser is connected to the new location automatically.)

302   Requested resource found, but at a different URL.

400   Error in request syntax.

401   Request requires an authorisation field. (This is used on web sites where a password or some form of authentication is needed before access can be granted.)

402   The requested operation costs money. (This is for websites which charge for the information on their pages. Before access is granted they have to know who to charge.)

403   Request for forbidden resource denied. (The website is off-limits to the general public.)

404   Requested resource not found.

500   The server has encountered an internal error. (The computer being connected to has developed a problem and cannot complete the connection. Try again later.)

501   Request denied because server does not support transaction method. (There is a mis-match between the Browser software and the software on the web page.)

Error Code 404

Of all these error codes by far the most common is 404 which is also one of the few that can be worked around - always assuming the website has not simply ceased to exist. Everything else can be fixed although it would help to explain the difference between web names as they appear in the press and as they appear in a Browser.

Whenever a company advertises its URL it will take the form of something like WWW.COMPANY.COM, but on the Internet itself such names are more likely to be, perhaps, WWW.COMPANY.COM/ SOMETHING/ SOMETHINGELSE/. All this really means is that the website is split up into several directories (also known as domains) which could themselves have sub-directories, each one holding different files. Typically this would be to separate different sets of information into logical groupings with the forward slash (/) being there to signify the different directories. Under this system the URL of the website as a whole is simply the part that ends .com or .co.uk or something similar. The URL of a particular page on that website is the complete path to it including all directories and sub-directories. (The names that are separated by a forward slash.)

Knowing this it becomes easy to work around error code 404. Start by entering the URL for the website as a whole (The .com or .co.uk name). If that produces the error code the website is no longer in existence so stop looking. However if this does give access to a website the easiest way of solving the problem is to use the links built into it to navigate to the right page. At which point the Browser will display the long and complicated web page URL. Should this not be possible, or just not obvious, and there are sites where this is true then add the next directory name to the URL in the Browser and repeat the process. Here a little bit of care has to be taken as sometimes entering one name into a Browser causes it to delete the name that was there previously, which in this case means the URL of the website itself. Usually this can be prevented by moving the cursor to the point where the next directory is to be entered and clicking the left mouse button. The next directory can then be safely entered (but remember to include the forward slash).

Copying Information

Once that website full of relevant information has been found it obviously makes sense to copy that information into some other application so it will not vanish as soon as a different URL is entered into the Browser. This can be done very easily by simply highlighting the text concerned, in exactly the same way that text is highlighted in a word processor or spreadsheet, and choosing COPY from the EDIT menu. It can then be pasted directly into any other application, although not always by the use of the PASTE command.

Very often a better way is to use the PASTE SPECIAL command which can be found in such things as Windows WordPad and then, from the choices offered, select unformatted text. It can then be pasted in the normal way. (Into WordPad at least, but from there it can be easily transferred using the standard copy and paste routines.)

Because of this a good tip is to launch a text editor, like WordPad, before going on-line and then select the run minimised option. This way if text needs to be copied the text editor can be brought up literally at the click of a mouse.

◆ While this is useful for small amounts of text a whole web page full of information should be handled differently. Here from the FILE menu choose SAVE AS and it will be automatically copied to disk either as text or still in its HTML format. Unfortunately this will not save pictures which can only by done by clicking on the image concerned with the right mouse button and choosing the SAVE IMAGE AS or SAVE PICTURE AS option from the menu that appears.

◆ Also keep in mind that where a web page is split up into several different windows, otherwise known as frames, each frame must be saved separately. To save a particular frame click somewhere inside it which activates that frame and then choose the save option.

◆ Where the information being presented is in a tabular format, like a spreadsheet, it should still be saved as a text file. After that use the OPEN command from the FILE menu of any spreadsheet and in the FILES OF TYPE box select text files. After that select 'fixed width' and information can be taken straight from a web page and placed into a spreadsheet for further calculation. Easy to do, but definitely something to boast about.

◆ Of course, an alternative to all of this is to simply print out the web page although even here there can be problems as sometimes the print out can be a blank sheet of paper. This happens when the text on the web page is white against a dark background and so, as backgrounds are not printed out, the printer tries to print white text against a white background which results in a blank page. To avoid this use the PAGE SETUP option in the File menu and from there put a tick in the box marked BLACK TEXT.

Although there will inevitably be a period of learning the techniques as outlined above should soon have anybody searching the Internet with ease.

Better yet they should have the same people actually finding the useful and informative websites amongst the strange, bizarre and downright useless sites that litter the Internet. By itself that should be enough, but for those who want more now is the time to consider the special problems posed by email.

email

As mentioned previously the informal nature of email together with the lack of visual clues can mean that offence is taken where a joke was intended. This is, or should be, of concern to any manager although here the problem is widely recognised by the whole of the Internet community so that rough and ready solutions do exist. As these go back to the days long before there were such things as Browsers, or even the World Wide Web, they are hardly sophisticated, but they work which is the main point in their favour. More than that they now form part of the conventions of the Internet which means they have to be followed if only so online messages can be understood.

Conventions

The first of these is a line or two of text at the bottom of each email known as a sig. Again as previously mentioned most email packages provide the facility to add these automatically so the only real problem is in deciding what those lines of text should say.

One good idea is to make them some form of disclaimer stating that the views expressed are personal and do not necessarily reflect the views of the company. Another could be the name, telephone number and postal address of the person sending the email while a third option could be some form of humorous quotation or joke. For obvious reasons this last option tends to be more popular with individuals sending messages from home than with commercial organisations, but it could be done just as easily. The only difference being that if the joke backfires it is the company who would suffer not the individual so establishing a corporate policy on the use of sigs is highly recommended. Should that be a problem then keep in mind that the use of sigs is not compulsory. They are there only to personalise a very impersonal communications medium.

What is practically compulsory is the use of certain acronyms sometimes referred to as Cyberslang. Initially these were introduced to save people with only limited keyboard skills from having to type long sentences although they have now developed a life of their own to the point where some of the more popular terms are now appearing in everyday conversation (the spoken kind). Because of this email messages are almost guaranteed to include at least some of the following:

AFAICT	As Far As I Can Tell
AFAIK	As Far As IKnow
AIUI	As I Understand It
BTW	By The Way
FWIW	For What It's Worth
FYI	For Your Information
IIRC	If I Recall Correctly
IMHO	In My Humble Opinion
IMVHO	In My Very Humble Opinion
ISTM	It Seems To Me
ISTR	I Seem To Recall
IYSWIM	If You See What I Mean
OTOH	On The Other Hand
TIA	Thanks In Advance
TPTB	The Powers That Be

A subset of these acronyms are used to indicate when a particular comment should not be taken too seriously. Usually they are placed in brackets immediately after the offending comment and can be any one of:

D,RFC	Ducks, Runs For Cover
<G>	Grin
LOL	Laughs Out Loud
ROFL	Rolls On Floor Laughing
<S>	Smiles

By way of completeness something other than acronyms can be used - and frequently are. These are knows as smileys or emoticons which are created by using the punctuation symbols on the keyboard and whose meaning only becomes clear after they have been tilted through ninety degrees. The most popular are:

:-)	Happy
:-(	Unhappy
:-/	Mixed emotions
>:(	Angry
(:-&	Angry (Alternative)
'-)	Wink
(:-...	Heartbroken
(:-#	Said something wrong

Finally, one last point, be careful about how many copies of the same email are sent. Just because it is as easy to send thousands of copies as it is to send one does not mean those thousands should be sent. On the Internet it is known as spamming (after the Monty Python sketch: Spam with everything) and is most definitely frowned on. In this case with good reason because if the tens of millions of Internet users all started sending thousands of copies of every email the system would soon be choked into uselessness. At times the sheer volume of traffic can make the Internet slow enough to begin with, do not make it worse by sending extra messages for no good reason.

FTP

As good as Browsers are at reading web pages they are not so good when it comes to transferring large files over the Internet. For this FTP or File Transfer Protocol is needed.

FTP has its origins in the dark days before Browsers came along. In those days, when the Internet was used only by academics, universities stored massive amounts of research material on their computers so it could be read by all. And they still do. The only difference is, now the range of research subjects has vastly increased. That and the fact that free software is also available.

To gain access to an FTP site first look at a Browser showing an ordinary website. There, the address line will be something like: http:\\www.website.com. Gaining access to an FTP site calls for no more than changing that address line to ftp:\\www.ftpsite.com. It is literally that easy. All it needs is the address of an FTP site which, believe it or not, can be found on the website of any organisation which also hosts an FTP site. Just search the Internet for information in the usual way. The website will hold details of whatever can be found on the FTP site.

Using FTP is slightly more involved than that as, before the site can be entered, a username and password will have to be given. Do not be put off by this. For username just enter the word 'Anonymous' and for the password enter your own email address. Assuming the site is open to the public, and most of them are, that is all it takes. A screen will appear, looking exactly like the files and folders arrangement of a computer hard drive, on which will be a folder called pub. As this is short for public select it and every file there is available for download. Welcome to the world of information commonly referred to as anonymous FTP.

FTP also has one more, very useful, function. It is used to transfer files between the companies who create websites and those who host them. Any web hosting company will give its clients an FTP address and it is to this that any files are sent. Be they an entire, brand new, website or just changes to an existing website the files will go by FTP.

However, anyone who has the need to send files this way would be well advised to use a dedicated FTP program. They are free, they can be found easily (on the Internet) and they will do a better job than an all-purpose Browser. No matter what the job it is always easier when the right tools are used.

USENET

Derived from Users Network this is, again, totally separate from the WWW. Briefly, the Internet is also home to what are called news groups which are broadly divided into several categories and which cater for every topic imaginable.

These categories are:

ALT	Alternative topics to those in other categories
COMP	Computers
MISC	Topics that fit nowhere else
REC	Hobbies and pastimes
SCI	Scientific research
SOC	Social and cultural issues.

In each case the system is the same. A messages is left on what can best be described as an electronic notice board to which someone else replies by leaving a message on the same notice board, someone else replies to this and so the process continues. (In Internet speak the chain of messages is known as the thread.) Although some of these Usenet newsgroups can be at the bizarre end of the spectrum there are also many which cater for the technical and scientific community. Quite often researchers can collaborate on a project, or keep other scientists up to date with their research findings, by this medium alone.

It is, in other words, a very valuable source of information.

For companies trying to contact those who might be interested in their products this can be an excellent way of doing it, but do not under any circumstances blatantly advertise the company or its website. Newsgroups are there to build long term relationships with potential customers. They are not just another sales forum.

This is a warning which should be taken seriously because the people who use these news groups have strong opinions about keeping them free from all forms of commercial interests. They are also more than willing to punish any transgressors so heed the warning - or find out what it is to be flamed.

For those who would rather read about it than experience it to be flamed means thousands of email messages sent to the company account. As these messages can typically be the entire text of obscure novels (which some people keep in electronic form specifically so others can be flamed with them) any company email will be lost in the crowd. At the very least someone will have to spend all day deleting the junk from the company system, and will very probably have to spend several more days doing exactly the same thing. Not for nothing is this also referred to as a mail bomb.

The Internet is there to be used so use it for what it is: a gigantic information resource. Any other form of corporate activity should best be regarded as coincidental.

Summary of points worth considering:

◆ Try several search engines and use those that suit personal preferences

◆ Enter any search term into more than one search engine

◆ Use more than one search term linked by Boolean logic

◆ When searching the Internet run WordPad minimised so information can be easily saved

◆ Consider using sig files at the end of emails

◆ Use acronyms (Cyberslang) and emoticons when a comment in an email is not meant to be taken too seriously

◆ Do not send the same email to more people than is strictly necessary

◆ To transfer large files use FTP - preferably with a dedicated FTP program

◆ Usenet is there so information can be shared - do not advertise on it

Appendix E

Governments and the Law

According to governments, and many private individuals, the Internet has to change. The only problem is no-one can agree on how it should be changed, or even why. Yet they all still say it should be changed, by which they mean regulated, and that it should happen as soon as possible.

Who Does What on the Internet?

The point at issue is the frequently anarchic nature of the Internet which in some eyes is highly dangerous, but which in others is part of its charm. Unfortunately those who see the charm are the net users, or netizens as they are known (net citizens), while those who see the danger are governments who are suddenly confronted with a global phenomenon beyond their reach, and in many cases beyond their understanding. For them everything from national sovereignty to public morality is at stake which is enough to exercise the mind of any politician even though the perceived problem is as much a misreading of statistics as anything else.

According to statistics of Internet usage prepared by capturing the search terms as they are entered into the various search engines (which, incidentally, demonstrates just how insecure the net is) there are three words which are invariably the most popular: sex, porn and XXX. This, according to the uninformed, is proof that the entire on-line community consists of nothing else but the depraved and corrupt who use their computers for one thing only. (The not quite technical term for doing this is one-handed computing sometimes referred to as left-handed computing.)

If this were true millions of websites would never be visited so how is it that these same sites are visited by the tens of thousands every day?

The Answer is Simple

All over the world people are joining the Internet to go on-line for the first time. It may be because their place of work has just acquired its own connection or they may be doing it from home using any one of the free trials which practically all the ISPs now offer. In either case the point is they suddenly have access to what the media keep insisting is the greatest repository for pornography there has ever been and, human nature being what it is, they want to see for themselves what the fuss is all about. Their only problem is they have only the vaguest notion about how to find it which is why they enter such obvious terms into the search engines. It may be the one and only time they ever do it, they may even stop using the Internet once the free trial period is over, but once that word is entered it becomes part of the statistics. There is no other explanation. These part time or temporary Internet users are affecting the statistics and in the process helping to perpetuate the myth of the Internet which is why they entered those words in the first place. (Those who do want to use the Internet for some left-handed computing rapidly learn far better search terms than sex, porn or XXX.)

Even so there are still many websites full of objectionable content. If anyone wants to see an artists impression of Princess Diana in the nude plus pictures of the crash scene the Internet is the place to find them. In other words the problem is real. It may not be as great as some people claim, but, nevertheless, it exists although what, if anything, can be done about it is an entirely separate issue. To be exact it is several separate, yet inter-related, issues which can be best understood when the history of the Internet is considered.

The Background to the Problem

When the Internet first began, back in the days when it was still called ARPANET, there was only one type of user: highly intelligent research scientists. Later as the Internet continued to grow they were joined by others, but the sheer complexity of establishing a connection plus the cost of the equipment meant these others were either students or professional people working for large organisations. As Browsers were introduced and connection costs started to fall the number of users naturally rose and yet still they could all be defined in the same way: intelligent, professional people better known as adults.

For a long time that was true; the Internet was an adults only area. It was during this period that the first pornographic or bizarre websites started to appear which disturbed no-one because adults claimed the right to have adult conversations. In America, where most of it began, this was even protected by their constitutional right to free speech. But then the situation changed; computers became household items, modems became cheaper than Hi-Fi's and Browsers were given away free. All of which meant the Internet was suddenly within the reach of everyone, including children which is the source of the problem. How can these children be protected from sites that could even disturb some adults?

The Issues Raised

Those who have been using the Internet for a long time claim that as these sites are already well established it is unfair to force them to close down just because a small proportion of Internet users are under age. They also argue that there has to be some places where adult views are allowed; not everything can be dumbed down to the level of a ten year old.

These arguments are valid, as is the point made that most of these adult sites require credit card details to be entered before access is granted. In some cases this is so a charge can be levied while in other cases it is simply an age check as only adults can own credit cards, but, for whatever the reason, it effectively bars minors from visiting these sites. Again this is a fair point, especially when software exists to monitor and control access to certain types of website which can be pre-defined by the user - or their parents.

On the face of it, then, the Internet community would seem to have a strong case, except web monitoring software is not always as efficient as it should be and websites with objectionable content does not always mean pornographic images. There are many other sites consisting of nothing but text, but that text could be anything from detailed instructions about how to burn down a school, or make a bomb, to software which lets them create their own computer viruses. From all of this children must be protected - if only someone could work out how it should be done.

The first point to keep in mind is that, with the possible exception of child pornography, there is no such thing as a standard, globally acceptable, definition of the term objectionable content. That might sound almost beyond belief, everyone knows whether something is objectionable, but not when national differences are taken into account.

National Differences

◆   In Britain there are many who would consider a website selling hand guns to be objectionable; not so in America.

◆   In many European countries a website promoting the use of soft drugs would be objectionable; in other European countries it is perfectly legal.

◆   In some countries pornography itself is legal.

◆   In many countries an anti-Semitic website would be illegal; in other countries anti-Semitism is practically state policy.

These are just a few examples and yet they serve to highlight the problems faced when trying to regulate such a global medium as the Internet. Unless every country in the world can agree on this, when they signally fail to agree on everything else, the situation will remain unresolved at least as far as international standards are concerned. In practice this means some countries are more likely to introduce their own regulations without regard to the rest of the world.

The Problem With Regulation

In many ways this is the main concern, not because of the confusion it would cause but because too many governments would take it as an excuse to implement a very strict form of censorship. Alongside pornography a great many freedoms would be lost. This is a problem not just for those who live under some form of dictatorship, quite literally everyone could be affected. All governments attempt to control the media in some way if only so they can set the national agenda which is something that can never happen completely for as long as the Internet remains outside the reach of an individual government. However, should that ever change then the sites deemed to be objectionable might just be those carrying political rather than sexual content. And after that many more governments might start doing the same (but only in the name of international harmonisation naturally).

So, to sum up all of the above. There is a problem with the Internet carrying objectionable or pornographic material. This is not as great as sometimes reported, but, nevertheless, it is still a problem. Steps must therefore be taken to rectify this, but no-one can agree which are the objectionable sites and, anyway, any attempt to curb them would more than likely result in political censorship. Also, just to add to the confusion, the governments who are leading the cause of Internet regulation to protect children are also frequently those who are spending vast amounts of public money connecting schools to that same Internet.

This is not a situation which is sustainable.

Fairly obviously something will happen. Even if no-one can say for sure how the situation will be resolved too many people are making too much political capital out of the Internet to allow it to continue in its present form. In which case the future could hold all manner of restrictions and regulations, probably introduced on an ad hoc country by country basis, mainly because no-one can find an internationally acceptable solution. (A case in point happened in May 2000 when the French government banned Yahoo France from returning the names of any Nazi websites no matter what terms its customers entered into the search engine.)

Legal Jurisdiction

One small step along the way might be an agreement as to which country has jurisdiction when matters reach the law courts. For example if someone writes a libellous email in Australia which is stored on the computer of an American ISP and read by someone in Britain which country does the libel action take place in. As it stands at the moment not even the experts on international law are too sure. In fact there is still a measure of disagreement about whether the ISP should also stand trial for allowing the material to be transmitted through their system.

ISPs and the Law

Unsurprisingly perhaps the ISPs frequently deny all responsibility. As they point out with thousands of websites and millions of emails being stored on their computers no organisation could guarantee the legality of it all. It would, they claim, be like holding a telephone company accountable because somebody made an obscene phone call.

In fairness to the ISPs there is a great deal of truth in that statement and to their credit they always move fast to cancel a website which is generally agreed to be carrying objectionable material. (An example here is the way the Virgin group removed a game that was stored on the computers of its ISP, Virgin-Net. The game itself was nothing too far out of the ordinary being no more than one character moving around the screen shooting at everything else in sight. In this case the objections came from the fact that the game was called Dunblane after the school which suffered an horrific shooting incident.)

A much more important reason why an ISP cannot be held legally accountable for the actions of its clients stems from the fact that if it was then that would also imply it had the legal right to monitor all the traffic passing through its computers. In principle this would be like a telephone company having the right to tap any phone line, at any time, and listen in to any phone call without the need of a court order. In short it would have more powers in that direction than the police.

As for the ISP's the more businesses, and governments, use the Internet so the less desirable it is for anyone to have the legal right to monitor what are likely to be highly confidential messages. It is also for this reason that the problem of objectionable websites has never been simply handed over to these ISPs. As even governments have come to recognise that would be a case of the cure being worse than the disease.

The Story So Far

Unfortunately that still leaves every single problem unresolved despite the fact that many powerful lobby groups are calling for change. At the moment legislative action is only being held at bay by vaguely worded promises that the Internet community is capable of self-regulation, but no-one can say how long that will last. Given that self-regulation failed as far as Members of Parliament and the City of London were concerned, and in the print media it is sometimes more honoured in the breach, what chance is there that it will work with all the millions of disparate Internet users?

So, expect change. No-one can predict what those changes will be, who will make them, when they will be made, or what effect they will have, but the chances are high that changes are coming. They may have an impact on the way business uses the Internet or they may not. Nobody can say for sure although for Internet users there will be at least one consolation. When these changes happen every last detail of them is guaranteed to be found on at least a dozen brand new websites.

To confuse the situation even further there is more than just object-ionable websites for governments to argue over. There is also the very unique problem caused by what was once the little known subject of cryptography.

Cryptography

As business needs a secure transmission medium and the Internet was designed from the beginning to be an open environment the obvious solution, probably the only solution, is to use some form of file encryption. In this way emails can be sent secure in the knowledge that even if they are intercepted no-one but the intended recipient will be able to decode them. Furthermore such a system is easy to implement as there are now many commercially available packages which are designed to encrypt all email messages before they are sent out over the Internet. In fact these file encryption packages are now so powerful that not even government experts, working with the most powerful computers in the world, can break them which is the problem - and the source of a great deal of heated debate.

In this case the objection came from the law enforcement agencies who are increasingly relying on message intercepts in the war against drug dealers, terrorists and organised crime. For that very reason they must be able to decode these messages or else lose a valuable weapon which explains their concern over such powerful encryption packages. At first they tried to restrict the power of the encryption to make the code easier for them to break, but in practice that proved to be unworkable.

While the law enforcement agencies could break the weaker code so too could others who announced the fact over the Internet. Not unnaturally this made the product impossible to sell, especially to the major financial institutions whose transactions needed security above all, and so the encryption had to be strengthened. Then strengthened again when that was broken. Eventually, with code breakers all over the world competing against each other to see who could be the first to break the next encryption package, the enforcement agencies decided it was time to try a different approach - and that was when the arguments started.

Key Escrow

The system proposed is known as key escrow which means whatever key a company decides on to encode and decode its material (in simple terms the password that opens the file) a copy of this key must be sent to what is known as a Trusted Third Party or TTP. Under normal circumstances this is as far as it goes, but should a government agency ever need to read those company messages a court order is all it takes for the Trusted Third Party to hand the key over.

In theory that sounds simple, practical and done for the best possible reason, but once the security experts began to study the proposals in detail its deficiencies soon became clear. Of these the most important was that anyone involved in drug dealing, organised crime or terrorism would hardly be likely to hand over a copy of their encoding key no matter what penalty was imposed.

In other words the system would catch everyone but the people it was aimed at.

National Differences

Because of this the idea was put on hold pending further discussions which is another way of saying every single government was free to take its own decisions - which they did. In America encryption software is classed as munitions and needs exactly the same export certificate as that for missiles or tanks. In France the use of encryption software needs the personal approval of the Prime Minister while in Germany the use of this same software is not only tolerated but actively recommended even for private citizens.

As for Britain its centuries of parliamentary democracy came into play and a commission was appointed to study the problem. This finally came to a head in 1998 when the Queen's speech contained proposals to regulate the use of cryptography by some form of key escrow. Exactly how this will be implemented is still a matter of some debate, and likely to be so for a considerable time to come not the least because in their election manifesto the government declared key escrow to be: 'wrong in principle, unworkable in practice and damaging to the long term economic value of the information networks.' Apparently the view from government is different to that of opposition.

How all of this will be resolved is open to question although, as can be seen, key escrow does seem to be gaining in popularity even among the governments who admit it is unworkable. As such it may or may not be introduced. Like the problem of objectionable websites it is something every government wants to talk about without actually doing anything, mainly because of the civil liberties issues every solution raises.

Even so in Britain current legislation means that the police will have the right to force ISPs to hand over copies of any emails going through their system which naturally means the ISPs must monitor these emails despite what was said earlier about how undesirable this is. To make matters worse it will also increase the costs of these ISPs by an estimated 10-15% and could therefore drive some of them out of business.

To some, then, it seems as if the Internet is just a collection of intractable problems while to others it is potentially the mechanism which will break down all national barriers and force politicians the world over to start thinking in global terms. That may be attaching undue importance to what is essentially nothing more than a means of linking computers together, but it has to be admitted the potential is there.

Of course, that would also explain why it is both feared and loved in equal measure although no-one can predict what the eventual outcome will be. Between the authoritarians and the libertarians the struggle is likely to be long and hard, not to mention fiercely fought. About all that can be said with any certainty is that the future of the Internet will be both fascinating to watch and frustrating to take part in.

There again, cyberspace was like that right from the very beginning.

Appendix F

Glossary of Terms

account To access the Internet, you will need an account on a computer that is connected to the Internet. This will allow you to access the computer. Your Internet Service Provider will provide you with an account. The name given to your account will become your userid.

anonymous ftp The process of connecting to other computers on the Internet which allow public access (that is, which don't require that you have an account before you connect) in order to retrieve files stored on them. Connection is established using the ftp program, logging in with the username of "anonymous" and entering your email address as the password.

Archie A service available to all Internet users which is used to search for files or directories on other computers on the Internet which allow anonymous ftp logins. Once you locate the file, you can download it using your Web browser (see below) or an ftp program.

ARPANet The origin of the global network now called the Internet. In the 1960s ARPANet was created for the US military, which has since developed its own network, called MILNet.

article The name used to refer to messages posted on the Usenet news system.

ascii American Standard Code for Information Interchange. The main printable character set used by today's computers.

binary file A computer file which contains characters other than pure (ascii) text.

bit "binary digit". The smallest unit of measurement of computer data.

bps Bits per second. The speed by which modems are rated. This specifies the amount of data a modem can send and receive each second.

byte A byte is (usually) made up of 8 bits. A byte is the smallest addressable unit of data storage. The size of a computer file or disk is generally referred to in bytes. A kilobyte is a thousand bytes, a megabyte is a thousand thousand bytes.

client A software program which connects to and interacts with another computer resource (called a server program). In Internet terms, a client program is a program which interacts with an Internet resource, such as a Web site or Gopher site.

dial-up Can be used in two senses: (1) The act of temporarily connecting to another computer using a modem and an ordinary telephone line; or (2) A type of account on a Unix host which allows limited access to its services (usually accessed via a temporary modem connection).

DNS Domain Name System. The system which regulates the naming of computers on the Net. The name and network address of every computer connected to the Internet is stored in a massive database which other computers access in order to translate computer names (such as domain.com.au) to numeric (IP) addresses (such as 123.321.43.34).

domain name The official Internet name for a computer connected to the Internet. Your email address is comprised of your userid and the domain name of your ISP's computer, separated by the "@" symbol; i.e. userid@domainname.

dumb terminal In essence a computer screen and keyboard, connected via cable to a central computer. It is called a "dumb" terminal because it lacks storage space (i.e. a hard disk) or a "brain" (CPU) of its own.

email Electronic mail

email address Your email address contains all the information other computers connected to the Internet need to send email to you. It is comprised of your userid and the domain name of your ISP's computer, separated by the @ symbol; i.e. userid@domainname.

FAQ Frequently Asked Questions. A FAQ file is a compilation of questions and answers, designed to help newcomers to the Net.

These can be found in Usenet newsgroups aimed at new users.

finger A program which allows you to determine if a user is logged on, plus other useful information about them (such as when they were last logged on and whether they have any unread email).

ftp (1) The file transfer protocol: the standard which dictates the manner in which files are copied from computer to computer across the Internet; (2) The program used to copy files from one computer to another across the Internet.

Gopher A menu-driven interface used to find information on different computer systems. Usually accessed via telnet or a gopher client.

host A computer on the Internet which allows users to connect to it.

http hypertext transfer protocol. The protocol which regulates how information is transferred over the World Wide Web.

hypertext Documents that contain links to other documents. Hypertext forms the basis of the World Wide Web.

Internet Service Provider (ISP) A company which provides Internet access.

InterNIC The Internet Network Information Centre — the closest thing to a central Internet organising body.

Internet Protocol (IP) One of the many protocols or standards which regulate the way in which information is passed between computers on the Internet.

mailing list A list of email addresses of people who share a common interest. When you send an email message via a mailing list it is automatically copied and sent to every other person on that list.

modem A device used to connect two computers via a telephone line.

moderator The person who scrutinises posts made to certain newsgroups, called moderated newsgroups, to ensure that they are accurate and on topic.

newsgroup The name given to each of the electronic notice or bulletin boards which comprise Usenet.

newsreader A program used to read, post or reply to news articles on Usenet.

packet The term given to a unit of data sent over a network.

PPP See SLIP/PPP.

protocol A standard which dictates how computers on a network interact with each other. The most important protocol for Internet computers is TCP/IP.

router A device which transfers data between one or more networks, ensuring that it is delivered quickly and efficiently.

server (1) Software which is used to provide access to an Internet resource e.g. a Web server. To access the server software, you usually need a client program. (2) The computer which is running the server software.

SLIP/PPP Serial Line Internet Protocol/ Point-to-Point. Two different types of software used to connect computers via modem. When you run either SLIP or PPP software on your computer to connect to your ISP's computer, you are assigned an IP address, and become a part of the Internet for the duration of that connection.

TCP Transmission Control Protocol. A protocol or standard which regulates how information is shared between computers on a network.

telnet A program used to connect to computers over the Internet.

Unix An operating system designed in the late 60s for large mainframe computers. Thanks to its flexibility, networkability and suitability for a number of different computer platforms, Unix became very popular in academic computing circles.

Usenet The collection of thousands of electronic notice boards or discussion groups where information and ideas are exchanged on an endless array of topics.

upload The act of sending files or information from your computer to another computer, usually referred to as a remote host.

Marketing Your Website

Shows you how to construct and deliver a successful promotional strategy. It covers everything from the basics of linking to other sites and search engine registration, though to referral sales and associate programmes. You will learn: ● How to promote their site in newsgroups and chat rooms without being flamed, ● The importance of META tags and how to use them, ● How to build customer loyalty, ● What is meant by 'sticky content' and how to write it, ● Ways of promoting a site in the traditional media,

£7.95   112 Pages   Tim Ireland

Creating a Website

Whether it is to showcase your business and its products, or a compilation of information about your favourite hobby or sport, creating your own Web site is very exciting indeed. This book will help demystify the process of creating and publishing a Web site. Includes what free tools are available, how to create dazzling graphics, using a variety of free computer programs and who to talk to when it comes to finding a home for your Web site.

£6.95   112 Pages   Tim Ireland

Understand Financial Risk in a Day

Risk management is all about minimising risks and maximising opportunities. Those who understand what they should be doing, as a result of their risk calculations, will usually come out as winners. Those who flail in the dark will, more often than not, be the losers.

Light on detailed formulae and heavy on easy-to-follow examples this book leads you to a greater awareness of how to evaluate the risks you are facing and adapt a strategy to create the best possible outcome.

£6.95   96 Pages   Alex Kiam

Investing for the Long term

This book is NOT about making a quick killing on the stockmarket. It is specifically aimed at helping you produce a low-risk, stable portfolio that will guarantee your long-term financial security. By using the advice inside and a little common sense you will slowly, but surely, acquire real wealth. It explains how to beat the professional fund managers at their own game. With the knowledge it brings, you will be able to run your own portfolio, thus avoiding the hefty management fees that can make a huge difference over many years.

£14.95 hardback   192 Pages   Robert Linggard

Be Your Own Spin Doctor

We live in the age of the spin doctor. The world's of business, showbiz, and most of all politics, are dominated by their activities. But dealing with the media is not rocket science, or black magic; there are ground rules and conventions, there are techniques and tricks of the trade, and it can be learned by anyone.

"A useful guide for all campaigners and communicators"
- Peter Mandelson MP

£6.95   144 Pages   Paul Richards

Understand Derivatives in a Day

Financial derivatives are used as highly-geared vehicles for making money, saving money or preventing its loss. They also have the ability to exploit volatility, guarantee results and avoid taxes.   But only if they are used correctly.   Learn...How private investors get started... To Hedge, Straddle and control Risk... Ways to limit the downside but not the upside... About risk free derivative strategies... Trading Psychology...   Currency Speculation; Long and Short puts; Tarantula Trading; and much more.

£6.95   128 Pages   Stefan Bernstein

Book Ordering

Please complete the form below or use a plain piece of paper and send to:

Europe/Asia
TTL, PO Box 200, Harrogate, North Yorks HG1 2YR, England
(or fax to 01423-526035, or email: sales@net-works.co.uk).

USA/Canada
Trafalgar Square, PO Box 257, Howe Hill Road, North Pomfret, Vermont
05053 (or fax to 802-457-1913, call toll free 800-423-4525, or email:
tsquare@sover.net)

Postage and handling charge:
UK - £1 for first book, and 50p for each additional book
USA - $5 for first book, and $2 for each additional book (all shipments by
UPS, please provide street address).
Elsewhere - £3 for first book, and £1.50 for each additional book via surface
post (for airmail and courier rates, please fax or email for a price quote)

Book	Qty	Price
	Postage	
	Total:	

☐   I enclose payment for £_____

☐   Please debit my Visa/Amex/Mastercard

No: ☐☐☐☐ - ☐☐☐☐ - ☐☐☐☐ - ☐☐☐☐

Expiry Date: ☐☐☐☐   Signature: _____

Name:Mr/Mrs/Miss: _____

Address: _____

_____

_____

Postcode/Zip: _____   Country:_____

netmanag